Lightning Path Workbook Three

The Basics

Version 1.0

By Michael Sharp

www.thelightningpath.com
www.michaelsharp.org

A life is either all spiritual or not spiritual at all. No man can serve two masters. Your life is shaped by the end you live for. You are made in the image of what you desire.

— Thomas Merton

I believe in God, but not as one thing, not as an old man in the sky. I believe that what people call God is something in all of us. I believe that what Jesus and Mohammed and Buddha and all the rest said was right. It's just that the translations have gone wrong.

— John Lennon

Lightning Path Workbook Three

The Basics

Version 1.0

By Michael Sharp

www.thelightningpath.com

www.michaelsharp.org

Published by Lightning Path Press

St. Albert, Alberta Canada

press.thelightningpath.com

Version 1.00

©2016 Lightning Path

ISBN PAPER: 978-1-897455-24-1
ISBN PDF: 978-1-897455-28-9

Table of Contents

Preface

Greetings and welcome to the Lightning Path (or just LP for short). The Lightning Path is a powerful, effective, grounded, logical, intuitive, modern, and authentic path of **Spiritual Realization**.[1] The Lightning Path is the child of Dr. Michael Sharp, a sociologist, counselor, and practicing mystic. It has been in development for over a decade and is designed to provide a fast path towards personal rediscovery of the deep spiritual truth of our shared collective divinity, unencumbered by oppressive structures, greed, corruption, profiteering, and ego.

The workbook that you have in your hand is book three in the Lightning Path Workbook series. This book is preceded by *Lightning Path Workbook One: Introduction to Authentic Spirituality*, and *Lightning Path Workbook Two: Introduction to the Lightning Path*. This book covers basic spiritual technique and concepts. This book does not stand-alone. It is part of a larger curriculum. See the Lightning Path website at http://www.thelightningpath.com/ for more information.

---

[1] Spiritual Realization, or just Realization for short, is the process of revealing/discovering/*realizing your* inner divinity. Realization is another word for enlightenment. See http://www.thespiritwiki.com/Spiritual_Realization.

Approaching Your Study

You can approach your spiritual study in one of three ways, informally as an interested seeker, formally as a registered student, or committed to deep understanding as an LP mentor. To approach your study informally, simply read the workbooks and other assigned LP readings, learn the key concepts, and answer the study questions for yourself. If you wish, you can organize workgroups to help you study. For suggestions on how to organize your workgroups, *and for study questions that you can use to facilitate discussion*, see the paragraphs on organizing your workgroup and study questions at this end of this book.

Second, you can approach your study as a formal LP student, with a view towards LP certification. For this, you need to register as a student on the LP site (http://www.thelightningpath.com/register/). There you get access to additional supports, materials, flashcards, quizzes, audio, and video to support your learning. You can get a complete list of the available learning supports by visiting http://www.thelightningpath.com/fast-path/.

Finally, you can approach your study with the intent of becoming an LP mentor or teacher. For this, you must register as a student, take the exams *and* submit answers to all the study questions provided in the LP workbooks. In order to register as an LP mentor you must complete the student levels first. To begin your study as an LP student and mentor, visit http://www.thelightningpath.com/register/.

Workbook Goals

At the end of this book, you will be able to:

- Answer four of the basic **big questions**.[2] These questions are, in order of ascending importance:

1) What is Spirituality?

2) What is Authentic Spirituality?

3) What is the nature of Consciousness?

4) What is the nature and function of your physical unit (as I like to call your body and mind)?

- Understand what it means to be in alignment with consciousness, and why alignment is the key to spiritual awakening and activation.

- Understand the basic nature of awakening, activation, and ascension.

- Recognize several obstacles, both internal (e.g. psychological and emotional) and external (e.g. resistance and indoctrination), that can block you and prevent you from moving forward.

- Begin developing and putting into practice several basic spiritual practices including intent, visualization, and deep breathing.

---

[2] Big questions are *big* questions like "Why am I here?" or "What is the nature of God?" See http://www.thespiritwiki.com/Big_Questions.

Key Concepts

By the end of this book, you should be familiar with the following LP concepts.

- Agent of Consciousness
- Automobile Metaphor
- Awakening
- Alignment
- Awareness Reduction Mechanisms
- Awakening Mantras
- Big Questions
- Bodily Ego
- Boundary Visualizations
- Breathing
- Cognitive Wall
- Connection Event/Connection Experience
- Connection Supplements
- Consistent and persistent intent
- Disjuncture
- Ego Explosion
- Forced awakening
- Intent/Will
- Monad/Monadic Consciousness
- Nadir Experiences/Zenith Experiences
- Normal Consciousness
- Old World Spirituality / New World Spirituality
- Old Energy / New Energy
- Post-consciousness Stress Disorder
- Right Action
- Rules of Alignment
- Self
- Self-stupefaction
- Spiritual Bypassing
- Spiritual Ego
- Spiritual Realization (or just Realization)
- Steering Emotions
- Toxic Socialization
- Visualization
- Wrong Thought
- Water Glass Visualization

Introduction

Greeting and welcome to Lightning Path Workbook Three – The Basics.[3] If you are engaging with this book then you should have already read *Lightning Path Workbook One: Introduction to Authentic Spirituality* and, *Lightning Path Workbook Two: Introduction to the Lightning Path.* At this point, you should have a good idea about what spiritual awakening is, you should have some idea of how to initiate it, and you should know a little bit about some of the traps and pitfalls that may slow or even halt your progress forward. You should also have a good idea of what the Lightning Path is about and an idea of the principles upon which it is based. If you do not, I recommend you track down both LP Book One and LP Book Two before proceeding.[4]

Once you read the previous books, and once you understand the basics of authentic spirituality and the Lightning Path, the next step is to familiarize yourself with some key LP concepts, ideas, and practices in this book. Some of these concepts and ideas will be new in this book, but some you will have already encountered. Here, and in subsequent volumes, we will continue to introduce key and core ideas, and deepen our

---

[3] Even though I use the term "basic" to describe this level, resist any temptation to jump ahead from here. It does not matter who you are, how much money you have, how many "degrees" you have attained, or whatever. If you are serious about awakening and activation, you must ensure that a) you understand the basics and b) you incorporate into your daily routines the practices and techniques that are provided. This is a critical step. The LP provides you what you need to handle the bright and powerful light of your own Consciousness. This might not sound like much to you right now. In fact, it might even seem a little silly to say; however, believe me, it is not. The last thing you want to do is "open the valve" and "blast your brain" with the bright and powerful light of your own higher Consciousness before you have the tools and the skills to handle it. Doing so will only slow your progress and possibly, particularly if you are dealing with trauma, damage from childhood, or external interference in your awakening process, damage your physical unit. If you move forward without a solid foundation, you may even get bumped permanently off the Path. I am not saying this to scare you into stopping. I am just saying, if you are going to climb a mountain, make sure you have the right gear, the right training, and the right mental attitude. Otherwise, you put yourself and those around you in danger.

[4] Look them up at http://press.thelightningpath.com/path/.

understanding of the concepts and ideas we already know. Ultimately the goal is a sophisticated, satisfying, effective, *and* practical spirituality that works (i.e. that connects you to Consciousness, that helps you realize the truth, and that helps you ground your divinity in your physical body). This is not a small job; this all takes time and attention to develop. Do not be surprised therefore, if you find me repeating important things from time to time or, equally likely, you find yourself going back to reread as you deepen your understanding. Authentic spirituality is simple but complicated, easy and challenging all at the same time. Getting the big picture might be easy, but fleshing it out, filling in the details, and engaging in the necessary practice takes time and effort.

Before moving onto our first lesson I want to remind the reader that there is an important practical aspect to all this. You can understand the ideas all you want, but if you do not engage in the practice as suggested, you will not move forward as you expect. Understanding the ideas while ignoring the practice is like getting yourself situated on the Path, but never taking even the first step forward to move yourself down the road. You may be self-satisfied with yourself standing at the beginning of the road, but do not fool yourself; you look silly and stuck to the others moving forward. Therefore, when you see practice ideas and suggestions, like admonishments to visualize or guidance on breathing or creating boundaries, take these seriously and incorporate them into your daily routines. Remember, if you are just thinking, you are not walking, and if you are not walking, you are not moving forward. Think all you want because thinking is a good thing, but do not forget to move. If you want to awaken, activate, and ascend, you have to do the practice. If you want to move forward, you have to walk the walk. It is just common sense.

One Foundation Stone: Alignment

To start this lesson booklet I want to look at what I consider the most important concept in the entire Lightning Path corpus, and that is the concept of **alignment.** In order to have a look at this concept, and in order to understand why I think it is so important, I want to take a bit of a roundabout path by first talking a bit about the nature of spirituality. I also want to talk, briefly, about what it means to live a spiritual life and be a spiritual person. Specifically, I want to define spirituality for you and get you thinking about the key components of a spiritual life. To kick off the discussion, let me ask you three questions, the answers to which fully define the nature of spirituality. Let me ask you,

- What does it mean to be spiritual?

- What does it mean to lead a spiritual life?

- What is the full nature of spiritual awakening?[5]

You already know, from LP Workbook One, that authentic spirituality is about filling the physical unit with the light of your own higher Consciousness. That is, spirituality is filling the vessel with light or filling the glass with water. This view is great as a general conceptualization and root for visualization, but it leaves many of the specifics out. In order to deepen our understanding and answer the above questions, recall the **automobile metaphor.**[6] Think of your body like a car and your Consciousness like the driver of that car. More technically correct, think of your body like a powerful red Ferrari and your Consciousness like the experienced driver of the red Ferrari.

---

[5] We will leave the activation and ascension components of spiritual realization for later.

[6] The automobile metaphor is a metaphor used to illustrate the relationship between spiritual ego as driver, and physical unit as vehicle. http://www.thespiritwiki.com/Automobile_Metaphor/.

Using this visual, you can understand what it means to be spiritual, what it means to live a spiritual life, and what the full nature of spirituality is as nothing more or less than the processes involved in getting into the car (i.e. physical vehicle) and driving it around creation in an effective, sensible, safe, and spiritually aligned way.

That is all there is to it!

If you want to live a spiritual life, if you want to be a spiritual person, if you want to complete the spiritual awakening process, then get your **Self** [7] (capital "Y" You) fully into the car (your physical body) and drive it around in an effective, sensible, and *spiritually aligned* fashion.

Of course, the million-dollar question now is just what is an effective, sensible and *spiritually aligned* use of the physical vehicle? To answer that question you first need to know what it means to be spiritually aligned, and that is easy. You can wrap your head around what it means to be aligned by again using the automobile metaphor. If you think of the automobile as your physical body and you, the driver of that car, as your higher Consciousness, then *alignment occurs when you get into the car and it drives exactly the way you want it to drive.* If you press the gas, the car accelerates; if you hit the brakes, the car slows; if you turn right, the car turns right; if you bank left, well, you get the idea. Your car is in alignment when it does what you want it to do and it is out of alignment when it does not. If you are driving in your car on the highway and you hit the brakes to avoid an obstacle but the car accelerates, then the car is dangerously out of alignment with the will/intent of the driver. It is the same with your physical unit. Your physical unit is in alignment when it does what its **Resident Monadic Consciousness** [8] (RMC) wants it to do. It is out of alignment

---

[7] Self with a capital "S" refers to your Resident Monadic Consciousness (RMC) or spiritual ego. Self with a lower case "s" refers to your bodily ego. For more, see http://www.thespiritwiki.com/Self

[8] Your resident monadic consciousness (RMC) is You with a capital "Y." It is your "higher self," your true self,

when it does not.

We can now return to our three questions concerning the nature of spirituality. Recall these questions:

- What does it mean to be spiritual?

- What does it mean to lead a spiritual life?

- What is the full nature of spiritual awakening?

With the concept of alignment in mind, we can say that *you are living a spiritual life when your physical unit is aligned with higher Consciousness.* You are living an anti-spiritual life when your physical unit is out of alignment with your higher Consciousness.

A question that emerges at this point is, how do you know when your body is aligned with your **Resident Monadic Self?**[9] To answer that question you have to understand the nature of the driver and in particular what the driver wants. That is easy to do when you are fully connected and when Consciousness has already descended into the vehicle. When you are in a state of awakened activation, "you" = "You" and you do not have to worry about it. When you are in a state of awakened activation, little "y" you knows what capital "Y" You wants like you know your own name. However, when you are unconnected you do not know what You wants and so it is much harder to achieve alignment. When you are unconnected, when little you "y" is not communicating with big "Y" you, you only have two options. When unconnected you can either

a) Consider what others say alignment is (hence the popularity of the ten commandments, self-help books, New Age treatises, and other attempts to

---

your "soul" if you like. It is the identity and Consciousness which animates your body and without which your body would be comatose and zombie like. For more, see http://www.thespiritwiki.com/RMC/.

[9] Resident Monadic Self is another LP phrase used to describe your higher Self or spiritual ego. See also Resident Monadic Consciousness.

specify/moralize about how you should live your life) or

b) Intuit it, infer it, or feel it for yourself.

I have to say here that it is always better to intuit for yourself. If you want to make the best forward progress, and if you want to inoculate yourself against spiritual rubbish and detritus, do not rely on what others say; get in touch with your inner BS detector.[10] Sensing your way to alignment is usually easy, at least once you understand what it is you have to look for, and once you are moving in the right direction. As I say in the *Great Awakening*,[11] follow your conscience. If an action (like for example yelling at your kids or hurting other human beings) makes you feel bad[12] then do not do it because it is probably out of alignment. The rule is simple. Do what makes you feel good about yourself. If you do that, you will be travelling a fast path towards greater alignment. It is that simple.[13]

---

[10] For more on your inner BS detector, see Michael Sharp, The Great Awakening: Concepts and Techniques for Successful Spiritual Practice (St. Albert, Alberta, Canada: Lightning Path Press, 2007).

[11] Michael Sharp, Dossier of the Ascension: A Practical Guide to Chakra Activation and Kundalini Awakening (Lightning Path Press, 2003).

[12] If you are reasonably psychologically healthy, these actions should make you feel bad.

[13] We are all naturally born with emotional mechanisms that facilitate alignment. That is, we are all born with the ability to feel good or bad about things, and so we all have the ability to follow our emotions towards alignment with Consciousness, even when we are disconnected. This ability to feel/intuit our way to alignment can be broken, however. In fact, it is regularly broken in men who endure a toxic socialization process that teaches them to disconnect and suppress their emotions. If you are a boy then the chances are very high that growing up your parents and teachers actually discouraged you from having feelings! Of course, a question that must immediately arise at this point is, why would parents and teachers do such a thing? Why would we break the ability of our boys to feel? Answering that question in detail is way beyond the scope of this work, but let me just say, it has everything to do with the System under which we live. In the capitalist/accumulation system that rules this world, traditionally it is the men who go out and work, go off to war, and run the big corporations. In the world of work, war, and corporate domination, men are often required to do things that are out of alignment with higher consciousness (e.g. spend long periods away from family, pick up guns, make corporate decisions that exploit children, dump toxic waste to preserve profit margins, etc.). If an individual with an intact emotional structure engages in these actions, they will feel bad about themselves. If they continue to engage in these actions over the long term, their bad feelings will persist and get worse. Eventually, sooner rather than later usually, emotionally intact men would clue in and stop engaging in actions that made them feel bad, unless of course their ability to feel has been

As for listening to what others say as a way to achieve alignment, that is ok as long as you are following good advice and guidance, but be careful. Do not follow bad advice and do not become dependent on others. As for following bad advice, I will warn you now, following bad advice and guidance is worse than following no guidance at all. Bad advice can get you so far off track and lost so deeply in the woods that you will never find your back, at least in this life. As for becoming dependent on others, my advice to you is, do not. I myself provide lots of guidance on what authentic spirituality means,[14] how to discern between good guidance and bad guidance,[15] and the specifics of alignment.[16] Even so, my advice and guidance is not intended to make you dependent on my advice and guidance. My advice and guidance is only there to get you to a place where you are confident following your own inner radar. Remember, the goal of good guidance is not subservience to a priest, guru, or religious system, but total spiritual independence and confident self-alignment.

To recap, you are aligned when your body (your vehicle) responds like your higher self (the driver) wishes it to respond. You are out of alignment when it does not. As for figuring out how to achieve alignment, that is easy. Follow good guidance or follow your gut instincts and feelings. Unless the emotional structures of your physical unit are broken, do what makes you

---

compromised. Thus, in order to preserve the System, in order to get men to do all the things that the System requires of them, a toxic socialization process is created that breaks the emotional structure of men thereby allowing them to engage in often horrifically disjunctive acts. We will talk more about the deleterious impact of the System on the emotional, psychological, and spiritual health of the individual in more advanced LP materials. For now, for more on toxic socialization, see Mike Sosteric, "Toxic Socialization," Socjourn (2016).

[14] See for example Michael Sharp, The Rocket Scientists' Guide to Authentic Spirituality (St. Albert, Alberta: Lightning Path Press, 2010).

[15] Also see Michael Sharp, The Rocket Scientists' Guide to Spiritual Discernment (St. Albert, Alberta: Lightning Path Press, 2011).

[16] Michael Sharp, Lightning Path Workbook Four - Foundations, Lightning Path Workbook Series, ed. Michael Sharp, vol. 4 (St. Albert, Alberta: Lightning Path Press, Unpublished).

feel good. If the emotional structures of your physical unit are broken, then you have what I would call **connection pathology.**[17] A connection pathology is any physical, emotional, psychological, or spiritual illness, usually arising as the result of **toxic socialization,**[18] that prevents an individual from seeking, maintaining, and/or establishing a proper, persistent, and healthy connection to Consciousness.

We will talk more about connection pathology in the next section and as we progress through the LP corpus. For now allow me to say that you are not living a spiritual life if you are not in alignment with your own higher Self. More importantly, you cannot go very far on any spiritual path if your body is not properly aligned with higher Consciousness. This is because there are strict limits on how much Consciousness may descend into an unaligned physical unit. If you are not in a state of alignment, Consciousness is blocked.

Of course, the question now is, "Why is Consciousness blocked if you are not aligned?" It has to do with the push-pull that occurs between the **bodily ego**[19] and Consciousness. Briefly, when something is not right, Consciousness pulls away and has difficulty descending into the body. Similarly, when something is not right, the body can push Consciousness away. When either the body pushes or Consciousness pulls, you are

---

[17] For more, see http://www.thespiritwiki.com/Connection_Pathology/.

[18] Toxic Socialization is a socialization process specifically designed to fracture attachments, undermine Self Esteem, destroy ego boundaries, and disable the body's ability to contain higher levels of Consciousness. For more, see http://www.thespiritwiki.com/Toxic_Socialization.

[19] The bodily ego is the ego that emerges from the neuronal operations of the Default Mode Network of the physical brain. The Default Mode Network are the neural structures that make up our self-reflective sense of identity.

The bodily ego can be distinguished from the spiritual ego which is the individualized identity/sense of "I" that emerges as the result of an intensification in the Fabric. For more see Mike Sosteric, The Science of Ascension: Bodily Ego, Consciousness, Connection, 2016, Available: https://athabascau.academia.edu/DrS. Also http://www.thespiritwiki.com/Default_Mode_Network/.

left disconnected and in "darkness," with Consciousness remaining at a distance. I realize this is a bit abstract so in the rest of this chapter I want to look at some of the things that can trigger either the body to push, or Consciousness to pull, away. Let us start with the situation where the bodily ego itself pushes Consciousness away.

Pushing Consciousness Away

As noted, when something is not right, i.e. when the body is not in alignment with Consciousness, the bodily ego can push Consciousness away. Pushing consciousness away is exactly like dimming the light in a room and going back to full dark. The light fades and you lose the awareness and sight that comes from the light. The physical unit, the body/mind, will push consciousness away for several reasons. The bodily ego will push Consciousness away because

a) It can't handle higher consciousness,

b) It has misconceptions (i.e. wrong thoughts) about the nature of consciousness and therefore cannot properly integrate Consciousness into the vessel, and/or

c) It feels guilt and shame at the unaligned actions it has taken.

As far as not being able to handle higher Consciousness, a few things can cause the body to struggle to contain its own higher consciousness. One difficulty is simple **lack of preparation** leading to ego blast and consequent psychological trauma. Consciousness itself is a very bright, very powerful light and its descent into the body of an adolescent or unprepared adult can be dramatic, powerful, and discombobulating, especially if you don't know exactly what might happen, and particularly if your expectations are out of whack with reality. It might not sound like much, especially if you have only ever experienced the day-to-day of **Normal Consciousness;**[20] but if you are not prepared for the descent of the Light, the blast can knock you flat on your bum. Some might get up from the **ego explosion**[21] and try again, but others may not. Some will develop post-blast stress disorder, what we might call PCDD or **Post-Consciousness Distress Disorder.**[22] PCDD is an irrational and unwarranted fear of Connection, arising from previous traumatic connection events, that prevents/blocks subsequent connection. A victim of PCDD will have strong fears and anxieties over the possibility of a repeat blast and this fear and anxiety will cause them to push Consciousness away. Fear and anxiety will lead them to shrink from the Light and try to forget. In the most severe cases, individuals may be too scared to ever return and try again.

Besides lack of preparation leading to ego explosion and PCDD, **wrong thought**[23] can also be an issue. Wrong thought is thought that encourages the bodily ego to push Consciousness away and/or that prevents proper integration of Consciousness into the body. I could provide many examples of wrong thought,[24] but the best example of wrong thought comes from "spiritual" teachings that portray God/Consciousness as a judgmental, vengeful, punishing, controlling, "father figure" who does horrible things to people who do not listen. When a **connection event**[25] is occurring Teachings that portray

---

[20] Normal consciousness is the average, everyday waking consciousness. Normal consciousness is what you get with the standard socialization processes of this planet. See http://www.thespiritwiki.com/Normal_Consciousness/.

[21] An ego explosion occurs when Consciousness expands into the physical unit in a quality or quantity for which the physical unit is unprepared. For more see http://www.thespiritwiki.com/Egoic_Explosion and also Michael Sharp, Ego Explosion, 2014, The Blog of Michael Sharp, Available: http://www.michaelsharp.org/ego-explosion/.

[22] For more, see http://www.thespiritwiki.com/Post-Consciousness_Distress_Disorder/.

[23] For more, see http://www.thespiritwiki.com/Wrong_Thought.

[24] And, in the *Book of the Triumph of Spirit* series, I do. http://press.thelightningpath.com/triumph-of-spirit/.

[25] A connection event or connection experience is the LP term for a mystical experience or religious experience when one "connects" to a higher level of consciousness. For an advanced discussion of connection events, see

God/Consciousness as violent/judgmental/abusive can cause an immature and developing bodily ego to be afraid of connection and to push Consciousness away out of fear or even guilt. Who wants to confront such a horrible and abusive patriarch after all, especially considering we have all done things of which we are not proud. Another example of wrong thought are notions that we are all "karmic rejects," ejected from the Garden and on a path of cosmic tutelage/redemption. Images of humanity as cosmic rejects lowers our self-esteem and makes connection with, and integration of, our own awesome power and glory difficult. When wrong thought has crushed our self-esteem, we cannot believe our own awesome power and glory and so, out of confusion and disbelief, we push our higher Consciousness away. In both cases (i.e. judgmental god, karmic rejects), wrong thought causes fear, doubt, and disbelief and these negative emotions cause the bodily ego, which does not want to feel these emotions because they are painful, to push away/shut down the connection. Simple.

So far, we have examined lack of preparation leading to ego explosion, PCDD, and wrong thought as things that can cause the bodily ego to push Consciousness away. A third thing that causes the body to push Consciousness away is guilt, shame, paranoia, and other painful emotions caused by misalignment and **disjuncture**.[26] As we have seen above, it is a feature of the physical unit that your RMC may invoke negative emotions when the physical unit is acting out of alignment. Negative emotions (and positive emotions as well) function as a kind of steering mechanism that higher Consciousness can use to guide

---

Sosteric, The Science of Ascension: Bodily Ego, Consciousness, Connection. Also see http://www.thespiritwiki.com/Connection_Event/.

[26] Disjuncture is the emotional and psychological distress that arises when the physical unit (your body/mind) is out of Alignment with You (i.e. your higher self). Disjuncture arises when there is a disconnect between what your higher Consciousness/Resident Monadic Self wants and what is actually happening in the material world around you. Disjuncture is an outcome of misalignment. For more, see http://www.thespiritwiki.com/Disjuncture.

a disconnected vehicle.[27] This steering mechanism works great if you pay attention and respond properly to **steering emotions**.[28] That is, everything is kosher if when you feel bad about something you stop doing it. The problem is, we do not always respond to steering emotions appropriately. This is because a) we have been taught to ignore/misunderstand our steering emotions and b) our bodily ego has the ability to suppress its own emotions and repress awareness of its bad actions. In these conditions, i.e. when we misunderstand, ignore, fail to respond, and suppress steering emotions, bad emotions accumulate over time. This can lead to the development of large caches of repressed guilt and shame. These large caches of guilt and shame can be a major problem when we move to connect. People who exist in normal consciousness are typically not aware of these caches because they ignore them or repress them. That changes however when connection (however brief) is achieved and Consciousness descends into the vessel. When an individual connects to higher Light, awareness floods the vessel/mind making denial and repression impossible. When Consciousness descends, emotions may rise to the surface and awareness will expand. When that happens, you become aware of disjunctive acts you have engaged in, you become aware of the implications and consequences of your disjunctive actions, and you become aware of the emotions that go along with these actions. Awareness and negative emotions flood into consciousness and can lead to the painful distress of disjuncture. If you are a pedophile and Consciousness descends you will gradually, or suddenly, become aware of the nature of your actions and the

---

[27] For more on alignment and negative emotions as a "steering mechanism," see Sharp, The Great Awakening: Concepts and Techniques for Successful Spiritual Practice.

[28] Steering emotions are emotions triggered by the resident monadic consciousness in order to help guide a physical unit towards alignment. Steering emotions include emotions like guilt, shame, anxiety, pride, happiness, self-satisfaction, and so on. See http://www.thespiritwiki.com/index.php/Steering_Emotions/.

horrific impact on the children and yourself. If you are a CEO in a corporation and the Light descends, you will gradually, or suddenly, become aware of all exploitive things you have done in the name of private accumulation. If you are an abusive parent, you will become aware of this fact. If you have psychological damage owing to toxic socialization, you will become aware of your damage. In other words, if the room you are waking up in is a mess, you will see the mess in all its gory detail. In cases where the room is a mess and there are large caches of repressed guilt and/or shame, the bodily ego may naturally react to the painful emotions defensively and push Consciousness out, particularly if the emotional/psychological trauma is very bad.

So, what happens when the bodily ego pushes Consciousness away? How does that look? One way the bodily ego can push Consciousness away is to use substances that stupefy, like alcohol, opium, or heroin. Intentional **self-stupefaction**[29] using harsh substances reduces the body's **Consciousness Quotient** (CQ).[30] Of course, my advice when it comes to self-stupefaction is, do not do it. Short-term, self-stupefaction may help with disjunctive emotions, but long-term abuse of drugs and alcohol probably leads to organic degeneration of nerve cells in the brain and CNS. Your body is a temple for your holy spirit. Treat it as such.

In addition to self-stupefaction, the bodily ego can also use various **Awareness Reduction Mechanisms** (ARMs)[31] to reduce

---

[29] Self-Stupefaction is the use of crown chakra stupifiers like alcohol or heroin to push Consciousness away, decrease Consciousness Quotient, and lower awareness. For more see http://www.thespiritwiki.com/Self_Stupification and http://www.thespiritwiki.com/Crown_Stupifier/.

[30] Consciousness Quotient (CQ) is a number between zero (dead) and one hundred (full consciousness) designed to represent the amount of Consciousness present in a physical unit at any moment. For more see http://www.thespiritwiki.com/Consciousness_Quotient

[31] Awareness Reduction Mechanisms are defense mechanisms that the bodily ego can use to reduce awareness of itself, its physical and mental condition, the "room" that it's in, and the condition of its life. For more, see

consciousness and awareness. ARMS include classic defense mechanisms like repression, regression, and sublimation, but also various forms of diversion and distraction, like OCD, compulsive shopping, and even long distance running. ARMS and distractions, of which I have listed only a few, help a bodily ego push Consciousness away when it doesn't want to become aware of, deal with, or otherwise clean up the mess in the room that it's in. We will look in more detail at ARMs as we progress through the LP corpus.

Finally, a body can push Consciousness away by a simple act of mental and/or bodily will. That is, we can push consciousness away by simply refusing to see what there is to see. Here I have in mind the person who, upon being asked to look at something they do not want to see, raises their hands to block the view, turns their head, and sings "la la la" to themselves as a distraction. Defiant acts of will may not be the most elegant form of rejecting awareness and Consciousness, but they do work and they can be quite effective.

Consciousness Pulls Away

I will have more to say about ARMs, avoidance, PCDD, wrong thought, and the disjunctive emotions of guilt and shame as we move forward. Before closing up this section on alignment however, we have to return to the push/pull of misalignment and disjuncture. As I have said, when we are out of alignment, a push/pull situation is created whereby Consciousness cannot descend into the vessel. As noted in the last section, bodily ego can push Consciousness away. In addition to the bodily ego pushing, higher Consciousness itself can and will pull/withdraw from a misaligned physical unit. It will do this for several reasons.

The first reason Consciousness might withdraw is simply that it

---

http://www.thespiritwiki.com/Awareness_Reduction_Mechanisms/.

does not like causing the body discomfort. As we have seen, when the body is dramatically out of alignment with its RMC, and when Consciousness descends into the vessel, awareness goes up. When awareness goes up, the body might feel the disjunctive emotions of guilt and shame. If the body is not in a position to take action to adjust behavior and re-align,[32] if it is in a situation where conditions are not conducive to change, then there is no way to reduce disjuncture. When the body cannot act, greater awareness is, quite simply, chronic torture. If you are aware of a bad situation but do not have the power to change, you experience chronic misalignment and disjuncture. Feeling negative emotions like guilt and shame over long periods of time hurts, and is damaging. In these situations, Consciousness will, in order to avoid exacerbating emotional and psychological damage to its physical unit, willingly withdraw to whatever extent it is able in order to reduce the psychological and emotional pain of its physical unit. This is a very important point, so let me repeat just to be sure you got it.

In disjunctive and oppressive realities where the body cannot make changes, Consciousness will withdraw to avoid causing unnecessary and ineffectual emotional pain.

Note, there is one very important exception to this rule that Consciousness withdraws when the body is stuck in a toxic soup and that is during periods of **forced awakening**.[33] Forced awakening occurs when Consciousness pushes itself into a body whether the body is ready for Consciousness or not. Forced awakenings typically occur at times of personal, community, societal, or (now) global crises, particularly when the survival of the physical unit is in serious question. In these cases, i.e. when the only possibility of survival is increasing the level of

---

[32] Perhaps because it is in an abusive and controlling domestic situation, perhaps because it is a teenager living in a hyper-controlling environment, perhaps because it is in a situation, society, or "brotherhood," that threatens those who do not confirm, or perhaps because it has "learned helplessness" as a result of chronic assault.

[33] See http://www.thespiritwiki.com/Forced_Awakening/.

Consciousness in the body so it can become aware and take action, Consciousness forces itself in. Notably, people often experience forced awakening when they "hit rock bottom" (i.e. reach the lowest of the low, the absolute nadir of their incarnated existence) because "rock bottom" is a point where survival of the physical unit is often in question.[34] At the point where people hit "rock bottom," Consciousness is injected into the body with force in the hope that, in the context of the current crises, it will generate sufficient awareness, realization, and insight to turn the tide and reverse the slide.

Unfortunately, forced awakening is not a pleasant process and it does not always work. By the time people hit rock bottom, many are so far gone that they shade into oblivion after all. I should also note, forced awakening could be quite dangerous, both for the physical unit and for those around as well. It is dangerous for the PU because it is hard, stressful, and comes at a time when the individual is at their weakest and most desperate. It is dangerous for others because sometimes the PU can snap under the pressure of growing awareness. When this occurs, and it will occur with increasing frequency as planetary crises continues to worsen, various forms of emotional and psychological catastrophe, and even violence, may ensue.[35]

---

[34] At this point, you might think that hitting rock bottom is a good thing. You might think it is a necessary part of the process. Indeed, there is a common perception amongst the people of this world that "hitting rock bottom" is some kind of necessary rite of passage. We hear people say things like "I had to hit rock bottom before I could change." Some even wear it as a badge of spiritual honor, but they should not. Just because some people are so sick and damaged that a death crisis is the only thing that shakes them awake doesn't make the thing necessary or even good. It is not. Having to hit rock bottom means the individual is embedded in a deep and serious pathology. As such, it should never be celebrated; instead, we should work to change conditions to ensure that nobody ever has to "hit rock bottom" just to wake up and transform.

[35] The reader may wonder at this point why Consciousness would force the issue when catastrophic physical violence may be the result. The answer has been stated—survival, both survival of the individual and survival of the species. Global, environmental, political, social, psychological, and emotional conditions have now deteriorated to the point where the survival of not only the human species, but of all species on the planet, is in question. In this dire end-times situation we all find ourselves in, Consciousness has no choice but to push, push, push. For more on the current situation and what has caused it, see Michael Sharp, <u>The Rocket Scientists' Guide to Money and the</u>

I would also like to note that forced awakening is never a good thing, nor is it necessary in the grander scheme of things. Many think that people must hit rock bottom if they are to change. Many believe that there is some kind of "cosmic plan" or divine lesson in the emotional and psychological crash, but that is not true. There is nothing in the dark night of the soul that is salutatory. Really, forced awakening is just a last ditch (and not always successful) intervention to save a body that is already nearing the end of the line. Rather than seeing it as something that is good, beneficial, or divine (i.e. part of "the plan"), we should see it for what it is, a symptom of the total failure of our familial, social, educational, and health care institutions. It <u>does not</u> just happen to people and it <u>is not</u> the result of personal weakness or failure. When somebody descends to the point where a forced awakening has to occur just to give the individual a chance at survival, that is an epic, nay biblical level, social, economic, and political failure. It is the result of years of toxicity and abuse, and a general evolutionary fail. It is far more enlightened, aligned, and spiritually/evolutionary sensible to aim at creating social and institutional conditions whereby everybody develops a full and empowered connection and nobody has to hit "rock bottom" just in order to change. As individuals and society, we will avoid a lot of unnecessary misery, and advance our evolutionary agenda far more efficiently,[36] that way.

Economy: Accumulation and Debt. (St Albert, Alberta: Lightning Path Press., 2016). For a spiritual look at the underlying plan, see Michael Sharp, <u>The Book of Life: Ascension and the Divine World Order</u> (St. Albert, AB: Lightning Path Press/Avatar Publications, 2003).

It should be noted that catastrophe and violence are not a necessary outcome of this last-ditch process, but they are a possibility. Notably, the probability can be increased or decreased depending on several key factors, including the state of the individual's family life, the state of the community they live in, and the state of the world that surrounds them. For example, an individual who has a forced injection in a broken family, a white-racist community, or a society with a politician that incites fear and hatred of certain groups, may snap and attack individuals targeted by their toxic community and toxic leaders. By contrast, an individual who hits rock bottom in a loving and supportive environment is less likely to snap and more likely to realize, shift, and make changes.

[36] Of course, at this point some of you are going to be scratching your heads in confusion here. Does not evolution

Speaking of misery, a **second reason** that Consciousness might withdraw is because it cannot stand the emotional, psychological, and spiritual pain of its body's existence. We have already noted that the first reason that Consciousness might withdraw is to avoid causing its own body unnecessary pain and suffering. Consciousness will also withdraw when it is feeling uncomfortable about the situation as well. Pay attention now because this is something you need to know. Despite what you may have been told, *Consciousness does not like negativity of any kind.* That is, Consciousness does not like to experience pain, suffering, exploitation, self-delusion, or anything else toxic/dark at all. It really does not! Consciousness does not find any salutatory benefit to struggle, pain, or suffering. It is not a "life lesson," it is not a necessary feature of the "checkboard," it is not something that "makes you stronger," and it is definitely not part of God's plan. *Pain, suffering, exploitation, self-delusion, and other forms of negativity are never lessons of any kind, they are* **avoidable** *pain and suffering.* Frankly, that is just what Consciousness will do—avoid! Consciousness, just like its physical vehicle, avoids pain and seeks pleasure. If it cannot do this for whatever reason, if it is too suppressed to create alternatives or if it is too stuck in a toxic space with no ability to get away, Consciousness will withdraw from the body as much as possible to avoid having to experience the negativity.[37]

It is important you understand this, especially as the "end-times" continue to unfold. Consciousness would, if it could, exit

---

= strength? Does not evolution = predation? Does not evolution = domination? The answer to that question is only "yes" in the middle evolutionary stages. At the advanced stage, a stage that the human race is currently struggling to enter into to, evolution = diversity! At an advanced stage, the more diverse a species is, the more it thrives. At an advanced stage, the more diverse a species is, the faster it evolves. In the advanced evolutionary stage, species advance fastest in conditions of **maximum** diversity, at all levels, biological, social, and political reality. Homophobes, xenophobes, and other "phobes" that react in a violent and suppressive way when they experiences diversity, please take note.

[37] This tendency for Consciousness to withdraw is captured in the 1960/70s phrase "buzz kill," meaning that negative people or negative situations "killed the buzz," "lowered the vibe," or, in other words, caused Consciousness to withdraw.

a misaligned vehicle to avoid profound negative experiences altogether. Shocking to consider perhaps, but it is true. Consciousness can shift vehicles like a driver can change automobiles. The only thing that prevents it from doing so is the design of the physical vehicle. By design, Consciousness is anchored in its physical unit and cannot leave until either a) the body can no longer hold it because of physical damage or b) the bodily ego cannot go on and finds a way to release itself from the pain (i.e. it commits suicide). Anchoring consciousness in this way is necessary because, as noted, the natural response of monadic consciousness is to withdraw from negativity. Without a forced anchor, many monads would simply withdraw when the going got a little tough. This would not be as bad if conditions were not as bad as they are on this Earth, and if we lived on a world where everybody worked together to make sure life conditions never got to "that point," but we do not. This world is, for a little while longer, a world of exploitation, oppression, poverty, and inequality; a host of social, economic, and political problems plagues the planet and causes incredible levels of suffering. Without the anchor, Consciousness would withdraw *en masse*. That would be bad because not only would it create a horror show where people regularly dropped dead for no readily apparent reason, but it would make everybody else's job much harder. Each person that exits leaves behind friends, family, coworkers, and responsibilities. These do not go away and the people who are left must pick up the pieces. For these reasons and more, the physical unit has hooks that prevent its RMC from fully exiting.[38]

---

[38] Of course, it should be noted here that just because the RMC cannot release itself directly does not mean it cannot find other ways to get release. We all know people who, in direct defiance of logic and common sense, engage in ongoing acts of self-destruction, like smoking, drinking, eating crap, and so on. It is very easy to find justification for moderately self-destructive acts and it is very easy for the RMC to *push* thoughts into the consciousness of the physical unit. If the RMC does not like its body, then in a bid to gain release sooner, it easily *encourages* the body in self-destructive pathways, thereby shortening the lifespan of the PU. If you are reacting with horror, I have to agree, it is horrible; but pause for a moment and carefully consider that you have probably seen

Still, just because Consciousness cannot entirely leave does not mean Consciousness has to enter in full measure. When conditions are bad and no improvements are forthcoming, consciousness withdraws to avoid feeling pain.

So far, I have noted that Consciousness will withdraw from the body in order to a) avoid causing discomfort to an unresponsive physical unit or b) avoid its own discomfort. A **third reason** that Consciousness might withdraw is when its vehicle is acting very badly and it cannot control it or stop it from hurting others.

It is important that you understand that Consciousness is the owner of the physical unit and as such, Consciousness expects the physical unit to do what it wants it to do.

It is no different from the car you drive. When you get into a motor vehicle, you expect the car to drive the way you want it to drive. If it does not, you do what it takes to make sure that it does; you fix it in other words. If you cannot fix it, you find another vehicle. It is the same with Consciousness. As Consciousness enters the vehicle, it puts pressure on the vehicle to act in alignment. If the physical vehicle is healthy and functioning properly, and in particular if the bodily ego is transparent to, and in alignment with, Consciousness, the vehicle responds easily and exactly to the will of its animating spirit (its RMC). If it does that, everything is OK. If the vehicle does not respond to the will of its animating spirit, it is problematic. If the misalignment is bad, and if the vehicle goes around using its venal powers and abilities to hurt and exploit others (if, in other words, the vehicle is careening about the road smashing into everything around it), Consciousness

---

this with your own eyes. We all know people who, in direct defiance of logic and common sense, engage in ongoing acts of self-destruction. When we see this phenomenon, we all ask the question "Why do they act that way?" This is the answer, or at least part of the answer, or at least one possible theory. *People engage in self-destructive behaviors because their souls are looking for a quicker release from a bad situation.* If you do find this hard to accept and horrifying, good. Do not accept this reality and use that horror as motivation; quit wasting your time in selfish pursuits and do something to improve planetary conditions so this does not occur to you, your loved ones, or anybody else on this planet, ever again.

withdraws. If it could, if there were no anchors, it would exit completely in order to prevent ongoing damage, but it cannot. So, in situations when the bodily ego dominates the psyche of the individual and commands the vehicle in rank misalignment, and in particular when Consciousness has no influence on the physical unit, Consciousness backs away and/or looks for ways to foreshorten the lifespan. It does this for the same reasons it backs away from intense negativity, because it cannot abide the disjuncture.

Finally, in addition to its own personal discomfort, the discomfort of the physical unit, or its inability to prevent its physical vehicle from crashing around the road, a **fourth reason** why Consciousness might withdraw is that it wants to prevent its body from garnering power and insight from Consciousness itself. If the body is out of alignment and doing bad things, for example if it is focused on profit to the exclusion of human and/or planetary welfare, and if Consciousness has no influence, then Consciousness may withdraw to avoid giving the physical unit additional insight and awareness that it may use to refine its exploitative and inhumane methods. If this strikes you as an odd thing to say, just remember the body is nothing more than a vehicle. If you were driving a vehicle down the road and it suddenly started veering into pedestrians and smashing other vehicles, the first thing you would probably do is turn it off so it did not have the power to do more damage. You would reach up, flip off the ignition, and let the vehicle coast to the side of the road. That is what Consciousness will do when its physical unit is misbehaving. It cannot turn the power totally off, but it can power down and withdraw to avoid giving its misbehaving physical unit additional power and support.[39]

---

[39] Unfortunately, powering down does not always work because there are ways for the bodily ego to force connection if it decides it wants to. It can use **connection supplements** for example, or it can use symbols and engage in rituals designed to facilitate temporary connection. A connection supplement is a substance that facilitates connection with higher Consciousness. These include LSD, Ketamine, and even cannabis (esp. of the sativa variety). Connection supplements are the most efficient way to force connection, but either way works. For

Preparation

In this chapter, we have discussed alignment and the push/pull that occurs when physical, emotional, psychological, social, and political conditions are less than ideal. A question that naturally emerges at this point is, "What do you do to prevent/eliminate/overcome the push-pull of disjuncture?" The answer to that question is preparation! Specifically,

1. Prepare yourself mentally and emotionally for the descent of Consciousness so you know what to expect and how to handle connection when it happens.

2. Correct any wrong thoughts that may have seeped into your bodily consciousness so that your bodily ego and spiritual ego do not engage in conceptual/ideological struggles.

3. Align your life space with your own higher Consciousness so Consciousness can find no reason to withdraw.

As for preparing yourself mentally and emotionally, this process you are already engaged in. This LP book series, specifically books one through four, along with the additional books referenced[40] provide the psychological and emotional groundwork that facilitates your mental and emotional preparation.

As for correcting any wrong thought that might keep you disconnected, misaligned, and confused, this process you have already begun as well. From the moment you set foot onto the Lightning Path you have been learning concepts and ideas that

---

more on connection supplements, see http://www.thespiritwiki.com/Connection_Supplement/.

[40] Specifically, The Great Awakening: Concepts and Techniques for Successful Spiritual Guidance, The Rocket Scientists Guide to Authentic Spirituality, The Rocket Scientists Guide to Discernment, and The Rocket Scientists Guide to Money and the Economy.

facilitate understanding, insight, and, ultimately, connection. Providing you with a new conceptual structure is helping you to establish what I call **right thought**. Right thought is thought that supports spiritual awakening and connection.[41] I have to say however, there is much more to establishing right thought than is contained in these introductory materials. The process of establishing right thought can be challenging, particularly since to accomplish it you have to delve deep into the spiritual **archetypes**[42] and ideology that have penetrated into your bodily consciousness. In order to facilitate the intellectual/archetypal exegesis I have created the *Book of the Triumph of Series* as LP resources. These intermediate materials, which come after you have completed the basic level training (i.e. LP workbooks one through four), provide a detailed analysis of the spiritual archetypes of this planet, as well as guidance on replacing limiting **old energy archetypes**[43] with expansive and emancipatory **new energy archetypes.**[44] You can find out more about the Book of the Triumph of Spirit series by visiting the series website at http://thelightningpath.com/triumph-of-spirit/.

Finally, as for aligning your life space, obviously, do not do anything that is out of alignment. In other words, engage in **right action** at all times. Right action is action/behavior that is aligned with higher Consciousness and that supports Connection. If you do not do anything that is out of alignment with your own higher self, you will not create the conditions for disjuncture, and you will not end up in a position where you find yourself pushing and pulling away. Of course, the important question

---

[41] For more see http://www.thespiritwiki.com/Right_Thought

[42] An archetype is any conscious or unconscious idea that provides an individual with an acceptable answer to a big question. See http://www.thespiritwiki.com/Archetypes

[43] Old energy archetypes are archetypes designed to disconnect the bodily ego from Consciousness and deactivate/damage the physical unit. http://www.thespiritwiki.com/Old_Energy_Archetypes

[44] New energy archetypes are archetypes whose creative intent is the awakening, activation, and ascension of the planet. http://www.thespiritwiki.com/New_Energy_Archetypes

now is, how do you act in alignment? That is easy, at least to specify. Just follow the three simple **Rules of Alignment**. The three rules of alignment are [45]

1. Rule One: Do not hurt yourself, because hurting yourself undermines your body's ability to contain Consciousness.

2. Rule Two: Do not hurt others, because hurting others undermines their ability to contain Consciousness, and throws your own bodily ego out of alignment.

3. Rule Three: Do what you came here to do. Find your life's purpose, because you will not be expressing your highest Self until you do.

That is all there is to it. If you follow these three simple rules, you will achieve alignment. Now, having said this there are a few things I have to say. **The first thing** I want to say is this: following these rules can be hard. I am advising you to avoid violence of any kind, for any reason. This means no emotional, psychological, spiritual, or physical violence aimed at either others or yourself. Of course, attaining this lofty goal can be quite a challenge. For one thing, the vast majority of us are subject to incredible violence throughout our lifespan. We learn patterns of violence from our parents and teachers, we internalize these and model these, and unless we change our programming, we act these out throughout our life. Not only that, but we live in familial, social, political, and economic situations that frame and support violence as a means to an end. Our media glorifies violence,[46] our political system uses horrific violence to achieve its political ends, and our predatory economies depend on ongoing physical, emotional,

---

[45] See http://www.thespiritwiki.com/Rules_of_Alignment

[46] I think specifically here of the Marvel movie series which is nothing but a long, tiresome paean to beating up bad guys. Apparently, as long as you wear the right costumes, it is ok to annihilate other living beings. Of course, the Marvel universe is not the only universe that features constant violence. Star Wars, Star Trek, and most other major motion picture offerings feature somebody beating somebody else up.

psychological, and spiritual violence to function. All this creates an incredible amount of inertia and resistance, and this makes it difficult to make the shift and do the right thing. Nevertheless, you are going to have to do it. If you want to be able to accept higher levels of Consciousness, you must be in alignment; and, if you want to be in alignment, you must do no harm. Hurting another person (and this includes hurting your own children) is not OK, at any time, for any reason. This includes those times when you feel justified in causing pain, as for example when you convince yourself that someone else needs to be punished for their bad behavior. Remember this: violence against anybody, even when that violence masquerades as punishment,[47] is not ok.

To achieve alignment, follow the rules; but be aware that following these rules can be difficult. Speaking of difficulty, **the second** thing I want to say in regards to achieving alignment is get help. It is hard enough to engage in aligned action on its own, it is even harder if you are not prepared, dealing with PCDD, confused about things, struggling with dark emotions, or damaged in some other way. It may be too much for you to do alone, so get help if you need it, and do not be ashamed if

---

[47] Note, saying that we should not be violent towards those we consider "bad" is not to say that we should not be accountable or responsible for our own actions, or that we should not hold others accountable. It is entirely acceptable to hold people accountable. It is entirely acceptable to have high ethical standards of behavior. However, accountability should not come with violence and pain. Why? For the simple reason that violence of any kind hurts, hurt creates fear and avoidance (your body naturally moves to avoid things that harm it, and fear is a tool it uses to do that), and fear and avoidance are exactly what we are all trying to overcome here. I mean, if your kids are too afraid to talk to you because of your willingness to inflict pain on them whenever you feel like it, or if a thief is too afraid to admit they stole something for fear they are going to be hurt (i.e. sent to jail), they aren't going to say anything. People who are afraid will repress, suppress, avoid, and deny, and these are the very definition of ARMs. It is OK to be angry. It is OK to be frustrated. It is not OK to lash out and hurt another person no matter how respectable you make it look (e.g., suits, gavels, benches, fancy Iron Man costumes, etc.). In addition, note this goes both ways. You do not lash out at others, and you do not let others lash out at you. If you are in a relationship where you are the victim of violence, you need to put a stop to the violence, or you need to get out. Again, violence hurts, hurt creates fear and avoidance, and fear and avoidance are exactly what we are all trying to overcome here.

you do. I realize that many of us have been mercilessly shamed into thinking that needing help = being weak, but that is not true. We all need help from each other at one time or another. I needed help for certain key aspects of my process, my wife needed help for certain aspects of hers, and you will need help for certain aspects of yours. Needing help is not a bad thing, it is just a thing, and certainly nothing to be ashamed of. Besides, these days we need help for everything. Even the water you drink is available only because others are helping to bring it to you. If you need help getting your lawn mower fixed, get help. If you are confused about your life path and purpose, get help. If you need some guidance on alignment, get help. If you note the presence of ARMs, get help. That is all you have to do. If you need help, find somebody you can trust, and get it.

Finally, **the third thing** I want to say *vis a vis* alignment and the three rules is this: take the rules with a grain of salt. Obviously if someone is invading your home, attacking your children, undermining your ability to thrive (like, for example, destroying the environment purely for the sake of private gain), you cannot just stand and let it happen. The reality right now is, we live in a world of unconscious "middle-stage" human predators, and these predators regularly seek to exploit, suppress, and harm. This cannot go on. They must be stopped whomever they may be (even family and friends) and wherever they may be. Seek nonviolent solutions first, but if the only thing that prevents someone from harming you is kicking them out of the home and preventing their further access, by all means, do what you need to do to create the boundary. You do not do anybody any good, least of all yourself, if you allow yourself to be oppressed, suppressed, exploited, and abused. Take action to stop that.

That is all I have to say about that. I will talk about all this in more detail in LP Book Four and ongoing, but for now let me just say, a) the implications are clear and b) you have some work to do. If you want to live a spiritual life, if you want to connect with higher consciousness, you need to achieve alignment. To do that, go over the things noted here and begin to make the changes you need. Don't repress, don't deny, don't engage in acts of self-delusion, and for God sakes get it through your head that living a spiritual life and being a spiritual person is not just about you and your physical body, it is also about the world around you as well. You can take care of your body and mind all you want, but you will never be blissful and comfortable in higher awareness while the world around you is a violent, exploitative, toxic soup. As long as the world itself exists in such a state, only temporary connection is possible. For awareness to expand collectively, globally, and permanently, the world must change. I know it is a big thing to say at the end of this unit, and I know that it is a heck of a lot of work; but remember, there are seven billion people on this planet ready and willing to awaken, activate, and ascend. We definitely have the human power to fix things. All we need to do now is clear away the obstacles so we can get on with the show.

In closing let me just say, if you are struggling with some of the materials in this chapter, relax. I am just telling you what you need to know if you want to continue to move forward. If your goal is spiritual awakening, you have to work on creating both internal and external conditions that support the awakening process. You have to create the conditions where Consciousness can enter the vehicle, conditions where the body does not push its own RMC away and where Consciousness does not feel like it needs to withdraw to protect itself or its own physical unit. You need to create these conditions because when the body pushes Consciousness out, and/or Consciousness pulls away, no forward movement is possible. It is like waking up in the morning; if you wake up, open your eyes, but then turn around and go back to sleep (i.e. push awareness out), you are sleeping, period. It is the same with spiritual awakening. When the body pushes away and/or Consciousness withdraws, you lose awareness and go back to sleep, period.[48] Obviously if your interest is in living a spiritual life and moving forward, you want to avoid that.

---

[48] One mistake you should never make is equating worldly success with states of high awareness. Just because somebody has a billion dollars and flies around in a monogrammed jet does not mean they are connected in any way. In fact, exactly the opposite is probably true; in order to be a billionaire flying around in a monogrammed jet, you have to hurt and exploit many people. If you hurt and exploit many people, even if you personally are not "aware" that you are doing it, Consciousness has likely withdrawn a long ago.

Two Important Aspects: Ideas and Intent

In the last chapter, we looked at the very important concept of alignment and explored some of the important implications, especially *vis a vis* the awakening process. The basic message should be clear, if you want Consciousness to descend, align your <u>s</u>elf with your <u>S</u>elf. In this chapter, we are going to backtrack a bit and take a more detailed look at intent. At first, this might seem like a rehash because we discussed, in a bit of detail, the importance of **intent**[49] in *Lightning Path Workbook One: Introduction to Spirituality*. In that booklet I noted that intent, especially as manifested in the form of an **awakening mantra**,[50] was a key to the initiation of spiritual awakening/forward movement. The discussion in LP Workbook One was just an introduction however and there is a lot more to say about intent. Here I want to continue our discussion by delving into this notion in a bit more intellectual and practical detail and I want to start by pointing out that *intent is another word for will.* When you intend something to happen, you will it to happen.

Intent = Will.

The easiest way to understand this is to use your hands as an example. Pause for a moment and think about your hands. Ball your hands into fists, close your eyes, and hold them out in front of you. Now with your eyes closed, open your hands. Now, close them. Open them. Close them. Do it a few times and assess.

---

[49] Intent is the application of the **Force of Consciousness** to manifestation/creation. When we intend something, we will it to happen with the force of our desire. For more, see http://www.thespiritwiki.com/Force_of_Consciousness http://www.thespiritwiki.com/Intent/.

[50] An awakening mantra is a verbal or visual intent statement that signals your desire to awaken, activate, and ascend. For example, "I wish to return home." or "I wish to wake up."

Did you make it happen? Did you open your hands? Of course you did. And how did you make it happen? You willed it. You put your hands out in front of you and you willed/intended them to open. It was as easy as pie. You wanted your hands to open, you exerted will, and like magic your will became manifest. It is easy and when your body and mind are healthy, you do not even have to think about it. If you want your hand to open, you make a choice, and you will it to happen.

This thing called will is a very important spiritual concept for a couple of reasons. On the one hand, it is important because will (yours or someone else's) is what controls your physical unit. On the other hand, it is important because will drives the spiritual awakening process forward. As regards control of the physical unit, just like your car is designed to respond to the will of the driver (that is you), your physical unit is designed to respond to the will of Consciousness (that is capital "Y" You). Your physical unit is a vehicle for your **monadic consciousness**[51] and you drive it by setting your will, period. If you want to understand how to drive the vehicle, you have to be aware of, and understand, will/intent.

Two Steps

Of course, the importance of will goes beyond just "driving the vehicle." Besides being important to basic bodily control, will is also important because *the application of will/intent is what drives spiritual awakening forward.* In fact, the application of will/intent is the second step in the process of spiritual awakening. **The first step** in the spiritual awakening process is to get an idea in your brain, like the idea of spiritual awakening. If you do not have an idea, you do not know what is possible.

---

[51]Monadic consciousness is the single point of egoic awareness that arises as the result of an intensification of Consciousness. For more see http://www.thespiritwiki.com/Monadic_Consciousness. For a complete explanation see Michael Sharp, The Book of Light: The Nature of God, the Structure of Consciousness, and the Universe within You, vol. one -air, 4 vols. (St. Albert, Alberta: Lightning Path Press, 2006).

If you do not know what is possible, you do not even try. Having an idea in your head opens up a range of possibilities that do not exist otherwise. This is certainly true with spiritual awakening. If you do not know that spiritual awakening is a thing, or worse, if you do not have a proper idea of spiritual awakening and are confused about what it really is, you cannot set any kind of reasonable intent/will because you simply do not know what to intend. It is like getting into a car when you are only five years old and you do not know what it is, what it does, or how it operates. Without the proper ideas, you cannot even start a car much less drive it. It is the same with spiritual awakening. Without the proper idea, there is no chance of even starting the process, much less seeing it through to a successful conclusion. Without the proper ideas, you never go onto the second step.

Once you have the proper idea, the next step is easy. **Step two** is simply the application of will. If you want to move forward towards **Spiritual Realization**,[52] if you want to "make the shift," if you want to awaken, activate, and eventually ascend, if you want to get off the sinking ship of the old world and get onto the shiny new ocean liner that awaits,[53] you have to will it. You have to have the idea of awakening (step one) and then you have to will it to happen (step two). Easy.

As noted in *LP Workbook One*, when it comes to willing spiritual awakening, awakening mantras are the spiritual tool of choice, especially in the early stages before you have learned about chakras, your body's energy system, and such. As already noted, awakening mantras are simply intent statements that

---

[52] Spiritual Realization is just another way to describe the awakening process. Spiritual realization is you waking up to your true Self and true purpose. I could say that when you spiritually awaken, you come to *realize* your true divinity. I know it does not sound like much here, but it is. Trust me when I say that it (i.e. realization of your true divinity) is a lot bigger than you might at first think, and a lot bigger than I can capture in a brief footnote. For more, see http://www.thespiritwiki.com/Realization

[53] Take a moment or two to read my *Parable of the Ships.* http://www.michaelsharp.org/parable-of-the-ships/.

direct your body/mind to move forward. Awakening mantras include phrases like "I want to make the shift," "I wish to move forward," "I only want the best information available to support my awakening," or if you are in a hurry, "I wish to move forward as swiftly and safely as possible." When you repeat these affirmations deliberately and often, you move forward with consistency and effect. Try it and you will see.

What I have said so far about the importance of will and spiritual awakening should be very easy to understand. Having the idea of spiritual awakening is the first step; willing it to happen is the second step. This is all very fine and dandy, but this is just a basic overview. There is much more to say. In particular, there are three things I would like to say about will at this time. All these things are important, so make sure you are paying attention.

The first thing I want to say is this: *While setting an initial intent might be easy, maintaining consistent intent/will is not.* In this anti-spiritual world we live in, it has always been a challenge staying focused and intent on spiritual awakening; however, nowadays, and thanks to the ADHD world of "smart" phones, Netflix, and Facebook, it is far worse. We live distracted lives and we get distracted easily. But, and pay attention now because this is important, distraction is anathema to spiritual will and spiritual awakening. When you get distracted, will fades and new formations dissipate. Without persistent and consistent will, the physical unit does not move forward. It is just like driving a vehicle. Will/Intent is like the gas pedal that moves the car. If you do not keep your foot pressed down on the gas, if you do not maintain consistent and persistent intent, the car stops moving forward. This is very important, so pause for a moment and make sure you rub this into your brain until you are certain you will remember.

Consistent and persistent intent is the key (or at least one of them) to the awakening and activation process.

It is not enough to say your affirmation just once and forget it.

For reasons that become clearer later on in your study, you need to be consistent and persistent. Ideally, this means constant intent many times throughout the day. If you want Consciousness to descend into the vessel, if you want to "wake up," recite your mantras all the time.

I suppose the question now is, how are you going to remember to recite your mantras? You can do a few practical things in this regard. One thing you can do is put your intent to move forward on sticky notes and put these sticky notes where you will see them. Look at the notes often and repeat your intent whenever you see the note. If you are mobile and cannot stick notes where you can see them, an app that reminds you will also work well. Alternatively, pick something that happens often in your life (i.e. opening doors, answering the telephone, sitting down for a meal, etc.) and use that as a trigger. Whenever the thing happens, i.e. whenever you open a door, learn to repeat your intent statement as you do. Once the association is established in the neural pathways of your brain, every time you open a door, you will automatically remember to state your intent. This will create many opportunities to remember, will help you speed the process of awakening, and will increase your chances of maintaining consistent intent.[54]

If you want to move forward, you have to maintain consistent intent. This is the first thing I wanted to say. **The second thing** I want to say about will/intent is this: *if intent starts your engines, intent can also shut them off.* This is important because this gives you control of the process. If things get a little crazy, if fears threaten to overwhelm you or if you find yourself moving too quickly to ground, process, understand, and transform, simply signal your desire to slow down by issuing a statement of intent. Say something like, "I wish to slow down because I need time to process" or "I wish to slow down because I need to find support," and things will slow down for you. As they do slow

---

[54] Thanks go out to Janet Finnegan for this excellent tip.

down, feel free to take as much, or as little, time as you like. You have the right and the ability to set the pace. If you need time to ground, process, and understand, please take it. It is far better to take the time you need to process and integrate whatever it is that you are coming up against rather than try to race to the finish too quickly for you to handle. If you move too fast, your progress may be unstable. If you move too fast, the process may overwhelm you. It may even happen that by moving too fast you experience so much shock and awe, or so much anxiety and fear, that you get bumped off the Path for years, decades, or even permanently. You want to avoid that; so, keep your intent persistent and consistent, but do take the time you need to process, integrate, rest, heal, or whatever you need. This is not a race and as long as you get back on the Path, you will be just fine. If you do find you have to take a little time off, just remember to start up again. It is OK to take time off; it is not OK to go on permanent vacation, not just yet anyway.

Finally, **the third thing** I want to say regarding intent and awakening, and this is important, is that this process of *spiritual awakening is not a process that happens just in your consciousness and only to you.* Just like willing your hands to open and then using them to, for example, cook supper, changes the world around you, so also does willing spiritual awakening change the world. When you do it, you set in motion changes not only in you but also in the world and the people around you. Spiritual awakening may be an internal spiritual process initiated in your Consciousness with an idea and intent, but that does not mean that this does not have an impact on the material world around you, because it does. As I say in *The Book of Light*, Consciousness is the root of all things. By that I mean we live in a conscious universe and technically it all starts with Consciousness.[55] In other words, Consciousness is the

---

[55] Consciousness becomes energy and, as Einstein pointed out, physical matter is nothing more than crystallized energy ($E=MC^2$). Thus, the physical universe around you is nothing more than a direct emanation of Consciousness. For more, see Sharp, The Book of Light: The Nature of God, the Structure of Consciousness, and

ground and the root of creation, big and small. Reality (with a capital "R") starts in Consciousness; change your Consciousness and your consciousness and you change the world.

But, within limits. Initiating awakening will have an impact on the world around you; but, you have to understand, and you have to remember, you are not the only mind, or **monad**[56] as I prefer, that is manifested on this world, in a body. That is, you are not the only sparkle of Consciousness that exists on this planet. I mean, humans are not even the most important species on this planet. We are just one of many manifested monads expressing and working in physical units. It is important that you understand, all properly aligned monads are important to the life systems of this planet. It is important to keep this in mind not only because keeping it in mind will make you a more aligned person, but also because it means you have to have reasonable expectations about what is possible, given the fact that there is other life around you to consider. Let us be clear, you are not the only spark of consciousness with ideas, will, and intent. Everything else with a spark of Consciousness (however small you might mistakenly assume it to be) has will and intent, and that will and intent is both important and impactful. Remember this next sentence: *reality is manifest as the result of our collective intent.* You have to remember this not only because your intent to awaken affects you and the reality around you, but also because the intent of others will have an impact on you as well. *If the intent of others supports you, your awakening and activation will proceed faster; if they resist, awakening and activation will move slow going against resistance and blockage they put up.* Always remember, you exist in a lived context and other beings are important. Consequently, these other beings have intent and will that will

---

the Universe within You.

[56] See http://www.thespiritwiki.com/Monad/.

influence reality, just like your own.

I know we are all used to thinking that we are "sovereign" individuals on a planet of individualistic expression, but unfortunately, that is not true. We live in a collective creative soup the shape of which is the result of our collective intent. This can be a bit challenging to wrap your head around, but consider the household in which you grew up. Your house, how it looked, what it felt like, what rules everybody lived by, in other words the reality of your home, was the result of the collective will of all people who lived there.[57] If one person changed, say for example your mother all of a sudden became OCD, or your father started to have an affair, that one change would have an obvious and dramatic impact on everybody in the household.

The intent and actions of one impacts, often in profound ways, the life spaces and realities of people all around.

This idea is important. You (we all) live in a context and that context is the result of collective will and intent. We will look at the impact that the intent/resistance of others can have on your awakening process a bit later in this booklet. For now, I want you to think about your impact on others. Keep this important spiritual fact in mind: if you engage an idea with will, and if reality starts to change, everybody around you will be impacted. Of course, that is not necessarily a bad thing. If an alcoholic sibling of yours all of a sudden gets the idea that they need to get sober, and if they successfully manifest their idea of becoming sober through will and intent, the resulting change in reality will be positive and likely welcomed by all.[58] However

---

[57] Of course, if you grew up in a patriarchal household, perhaps the "dad" figure used coercive violence to get his way (i.e. to impose his will and intent) more often. If so, that is a case where somebody who is physically stronger is using that physical strength to suppress the will and intent of others around them. That is not cool. This exception however does not disprove the rule, it just points to the fact that the emergence of reality is a complex outcome of will, intent, support, violence, and other key social, political, psychological, sociological, and economic factors.

[58] I say "likely welcomed" here because not everybody may welcome such a thing. People who benefit from the alcoholism of the individual, other alcoholics for example, or people who feed damaged self-esteem by feeling

change, even positive change, is not always welcome, especially when it comes to spiritual awakening. Indeed, *when somebody initiates spiritual awakening the result can be a lot like blowing up a bomb,*[59] it can have dramatic positive but also unintentionally destructive impacts. You cannot expect people affected by the blast to either a) like it or b) welcome it, even if it will lead to positive change down the road. At first, they will not know what is going on. What is worse, because of the toxic way we are all socialized and treated, they may not trust what is happening, they may be frightened, and they may even feel a little (or a lot) threatened by the change that follows upon your awakening and activation. Therefore, expect anger, resistance, fear, and pushback.

The question at this point is, what do you do to handle the impact of your awakening on others? There are three things. **First**, *take it seriously and be compassionate and empathetic,* no matter what comes at you. This is not "evil" you are dealing with, it is anxiety about change, mistrust of the world, and fear of the unknown. People resist, push back, get angry, and lash out because they are distrustful, hurt, and afraid. You are best off dealing with that in a positive and life affirming way. Unless you are prepared to just walk away from all your relationships and responsibilities (which honestly, in some very toxic cases, may be your best and only hope for survival, much less awakening), you're going to have to situate yourself in reality and work with the situation and the people at hand. You can go a long way towards lubricating your own path of awakening and overcoming resistance if you address their anxieties, resistances, and fears head on.

"superior" to the addict, may resist the addict's efforts to get clean.

[59] This aspect of spiritual awakening is expressed in the Halo/Sharp *Power* archetype. The power archetype shows the impact of spiritual realization (i.e. awakening, activation, and ascension), on the reality that surrounds. As noted visually in the card, the impact can be dramatic and discombobulating, especially for those unprepared. For more, see http://www.thespiritwiki.com/Power.

The second thing you should do is <u>not</u> stop. *Continue voicing your awakening mantra and continue moving forward.* In other words, do not let resistance and pushback stop you.[60] The initial phases of awakening and activation may be challenging for you and others, but in the end, it is better for you, for the people involved, for all people, and indeed for all life on the planet, if you keep moving forward. We, and by "we" I mean all life on this planet, cannot go on as we are now. We are rapidly reaching psychological, spiritual, economic, and ecological limits and if things do not change, increasing catastrophe looms around the corner.[61] So keep voicing your awakening mantras and keep moving forward.

The third thing you need to do, or in this case <u>not</u> do, is just blast your way through. Keep moving forward by all means, but remember what I said above, compassion and understanding for the ones that currently "stay behind" is required. They are not being left forever; you are just moving on ahead. Assuming they do not drop dead, they will eventually follow along. Just because they follow behind does not make them less relevant,

---

[60] At this point you might say to yourself, "well I would never stop moving forward," but you do not know what you will feel/experience until you experience it. You may get no pushback, you may only get minor pushback, or you may get major, even aggressive, resistance, in which case moving forward will be hard. I know one individual who started an LP activation meditation and the next thing you know their spouse was screaming and yelling for no apparent reason. The spouse did not know why, but they were probably experiencing unconscious anxiety and fear at sensed changes. When the one reacted like that, the other shut the process down. What could be done? They did not have a very open relationship and the spouse was not open to discussing the idea of spiritual awakening. This did not leave the one with any good choices. The choice was either leave the relationship and pursue a solitary path home, withstand the worst of the assaults, or shut the process down. Shutting the process down was understandable, but unfortunate because it meant delay for the individual, and delay for the family as well. Of course, I do not point fingers or blame here. We all do things for our children all the time and we often stay immobilized in the status quo because that is the apparent option of least pain. Until more people move forward, this is the reality: we move forward, we face blockages and resistances, we stop and we wait until things clear. There is no point blaming individuals here because this is done out of love and compassion. In any case, the real solution is a collective one, not an individual one. *If we want people to move forward we need to create a world where moving forward is not seen/felt as threatening.* The more we create that world, the faster people will move forward, and the less resistance there will be.

[61] Sharp, <u>The Rocket Scientists' Guide to Money and the Economy: Accumulation and Debt.</u>

less talented, or less important. If you think so, you are a victim of propaganda. Besides, this is ultimately not about you and how fast you can move, it is about uplifting/ascending creation.[62] Remember, you are not the most important thing on this planet, you are just one monad among many incarnated into this biosphere. You are important, you are glorious, and you are divine, that is true; but, so is everybody else. *Your awakening and activation does not trump the safety and comfort of others.* Of course, this is not to say it is not going to be a bumpy road, because it can be; but soften, mitigate, and smooth over the bumps as much as you can. The damaged sleepyheads deserve the same opportunity, respect, and support that you do. Like it or not, we are all equal in the eyes of God and we all deserve the same concern, care, respect, and support. Remember this:

Have respect for all life on this planet, no matter what kind of body it is in and no matter where it is standing on the Path.

That is really all I have to say about intent/will, for now. To summarize, intent/will is important. Intent steers the vehicle; intent drives awakening; intent controls the world. If you want to move forward, you have to intend. Do keep in mind that it is not always possible to move forward in your current personal realities and with current personal relationships. Although sometimes it might be OK to delay your own personal awakening just to preserve certain relationships and to protect children, sometimes you have to get out and stay out. Remember, toxicity and abuse damages you at any level. I will say it now and I will say it again, if you stay enmeshed in family toxicity, you are going to take damage. If you stay embedded and subject to damage for extended periods, then do not even bother with spiritual awakening because you will be too busy

---

[62] See Sharp, <u>The Book of Life: Ascension and the Divine World Order</u>, Michael Sharp, <u>The Book of Light: The Nature of God, the Structure of Consciousness, and the Universe within You</u>, vol. two - water, 4 vols. (St. Albert, Alberta: Lightning Path Press, Unpublished).

chasing your own deteriorating health and wellbeing to worry about something like that. You might not like to hear this, but it is the reality. You choose yourself or you sacrifice your life to others. Sacrifice is fine, when it means something I suppose. However, if you are trying to save a drowning person and you drown yourself because you could not pull yourself away from the desperate thrashing, then that's not a meaningful sacrifice, that's an unfortunate waste of life. By all means, show compassion and support. By all means, stay behind to help the ones you love. However, if staying behind means damage, disability, and death to you or your children, *get help if you need to and get out if you can.* You do not serve a higher purpose and you are not aligned with Consciousness if you let yourself get dragged down by the increasingly desperate thrashing of the people that surround you. If you really want to help, if you really want to fulfill your purpose, intend forward movement! Wake up, get out, and get yourself to safe ground. When you are awakened, activated, and strong, only then can you turn around and throw a life preserver to the ones now drowning in the dank toxic waters of the dying old world.

Three Steps on the Ladder

In the previous lesson, we delved deeper into the significance and importance of intent. There we reminded you that intent is what drives creation forward at all levels. It all starts with an idea and some intent. However, ideas and intent are just the first steps up the ladder, so to speak. Once you get an idea to awaken and once you set persistent and consistent intent to awaken, things begin to change. When change begins, issues, challenges, resistance and even pushback may (probably will) occur. You cannot just ignore this stuff and pretend it does not exist. If you are going to get through it all you need to take it seriously, face it full on, and deal with it properly. It will be a challenge, but when you are connected and aligned with your higher Self, you are strong, so you can do it. If you need help, get it; if you do not need help, that is fine as well. Just remember to face it head on.

I will have more to say about how to "face things head on" in subsequent workbooks. In this lesson, I want to move beyond our concern with intent and provide a basic overview of what happens to you next, as you signal your intent and step onto the Path. That is easy. When you step onto the Path, three things happen to you. These three things are what we might call *three steps on the ladder*. Completing these three things is the basic goal of authentic spirituality. These three things are

1. awakening,

2. activation, and

3. ascension

First, you awaken. Then, you activate. Finally, you ascend.

Awaken, activate, ascend.

In this chapter, I want to look at each of these in turn, starting with awakening.

Awakening

At this point, you are going to be quite familiar with the awakening component of the process. If you have read the previous LP workbooks, you will know that awakening involves drawing Consciousness/Light into the physical unit and then shining the Light of Consciousness all around. As you will also know, this stage is exactly equivalent to walking into a dark room and turning on a flashlight, or waking up from a deep sleep. You walk in, you turn on the light, and suddenly you see the entirety of the room. This much you already know. What you need to know now is that whether the experience of shining your Light is experienced in a positive or negative fashion depends entirely on three things: the condition of the room, your current state of health and wellbeing, and your willingness to see the truth. If the room is ordered, clean, and tidy, then there is no problem and you can get down to the business of awakening and expansion. If it is a mess, if you are a mess, or if you resist and refuse to see the mess, then there are major challenges ahead. If you resist seeing the truth, you struggle with yourself. If the room is a big mess, you struggle with the challenge of cleaning the mess. If your health and wellbeing are compromised, you struggle for the energy and self-esteem to transform. You have to tidy the room and/or fix yourself up before you can make too much progress.

As you might imagine, waking up to a messy room can amount to some major challenges. Do not fret too much about that. It is always possible to move forward, and you always have the wherewithal to do it. You just have to take steps forward. Even baby steps forward make a difference and lead to change. Since you always have the wherewithal to accomplish awakening, the big question is, how long will it take? More precisely, how long before the room is clean, you are healed, awake, and aware, and you can move onto step two, which is activation. The answer to that question is, "it all depends." It depends on how messy the room is. It depends on how long it takes for your eyes to adjust to the light. It depends on how connected and strong you become. It depends on the resistance and pushback you may receive. It depends on the damage you have to heal. Heck, as already noted, it even depends on your willingness to see and accept what is there in the room, right in front of your eyes. If you resist the truth, if you refuse to see what is there, if you walk into the room, turn on the light, see a mess, and switch the light back off to darkness, awakening will never happen. It is simply impossible. *Awakening is shining the Light and seeing what there is to see.* If you shine your Light but then cover your eyes so you cannot see, or if you switch the light off and go back to sleep, it is exactly the same as shining no light at all, which is to say, it is exactly the same as staying asleep.[63]

I will go into more detail about the process of facing the truth in Lightning Path Workbook Four and in subsequent materials. For the rest of this book I am going to assume that you have initiated awakening, drawn down some Light, are willing to fix your damage, have no trouble facing whatever is in the room, and are willing to work towards cleaning up whatever messes you find. If this is you, then it is time to learn about step two.

Activation

As I said, once you have started the awakening process, once you open your eyes to the room you are in, accept what you see, and begin cleaning up, the next step is empowerment or **activation**.[64] In the activation stage you gather your gumption,

---

[63] Therapeutic note: At this stage it will make sense when I say that in order to properly support and encourage the awakening process, the first thing we must do with our clients is encourage them to face, see, and accept what is in the room. We might call this therapeutic stage, **reality formation**, because it is in this phase that we help the clients build up awareness of reality. For more see http://thespiritwiki.com/Reality_Formation.

[64] Activation occurs when your body energy/chakra system is actuated and pumping copious energy. Activation can be a challenging, even dangerous, process so you want to be careful as you proceed and move forward. For more, see http://www.thespiritwiki.com/Activation.

activate your chakras,[65] and begin to take action to make things right. What kind of action you take depends entirely on the situation you are in and what you need to do to make things right. If you are mentally and emotionally damaged by your parents and teachers, you have to take action to heal. If your current environment is a roiling, boiling toxic stew, you have to take action to fix that, or get out. If your children are being bullied at school, you have to make sure that it stops. If you and/or your spouse are toxic and abusive, you will have to take action to change. If a pedophile is roaming your family, or if you yourself are one,[66] you will have to shut it down as fast as you can. Whatever the mess is, you have to face the mess, get your gumption up, and clean it all up. Activate/empower and change; there is no other choice.

Like awakening, activating in order to heal the physical unit and clean up the messes is easy to understand, even easy to initiate, but can be quite hard to implement, especially if the room is a big mess, especially if you are hurt and damaged, and especially if you are responsible for a large part of the mess. It can be overwhelming, you can feel not up to the task, and you might struggle mightily with the guilt and shame that often attends advancing awareness. After all, it can be quite difficult to stand

---

[65] For guidance on activating your chakras, see Sharp, <u>Dossier of the Ascension: A Practical Guide to Chakra Activation and Kundalini Awakening</u>.

[66] I know every minimally healthy person on the planet is abhorred by the pedophile, and understandably so. Pedophiles use the strength of their adult bodies and the intelligence of their adult mind in order to exploit undeveloped, underdeveloped, and/or damaged humans to satisfy their sexual needs. It is sick and it has to stop; however, do not kid yourself about this. Not just sexual pedophiles exploit children to meet adult needs. Children can be exploited and raped psychologically, emotionally, and even spiritually. Some parents use their children as emotional surrogates when their partners are unavailable. Some parents exploit their children psychologically by putting them in parental roles where even mature adults would struggle. Some use their children like some people use dogs, i.e. to protect the family, or to kick and abuse whenever they think they get angry and frustrated. And note, even if you are nice to your kids, you are still participating. Are you carrying a smart phone? Are you wearing a Bangladeshi made shirt? Do not be so quick to cast stones. Instead, help us heal and transform.

For more on child slavery and your smartphone, see Sanna Chu, "Is Your Smartphone Created by Slave Labor?," <u>iDigital Times</u> 2014.

up and admit, even to yourself, that "I'm a child abuser" or "I'm a pedophile" or "I'm an immature and egomaniacal bully." Still, you have to do it. You have to realize the truth (awaken) and you have to activate and clean up the mess, whether you made it or somebody else did. There is no other choice. If you do not, then it is like turning on the light, seeing a room on fire, and then sitting down to watch it flame out. If you do that, you will burn to death in the fire.

Of course, the question now becomes, "How do you take action and clean up the mess? "Answering that question is way beyond the scope of this work and so we will pick it up in a bit more detail in Lightning Path Workbook Four. For now, there are six things that I would like to say about the awakening and activation process that may help you stay on task and secure forward progress.

The first thing I want to say is, do not freak out. I kid you not when I say it can be overwhelming. No matter how good you think your psychological, emotional, and/or spiritual background is, the task is massive. It starts with fixing up your own self, moves into repair and healing of the family sphere (where possible), continues with you contributing to the repair and ascension of your society and this planet, and only ends when utopia is fully realized. There is no denying, this is a big task. If this freaks you out a bit, take a few deep breaths and know that we can do it.

Speaking of "we," **the second thing** I want to say, and this might help calm you down a bit, is "Don't do it alone." You do not have to do it alone. Even now, some help is available, and this will just grow over time. There are billions of people on this world currently in the process of awakening or actively getting ready to start, and no stinking "trump" card is going to be able to stop it. Once things really get rolling, once those billions start to wake up and clean up, things are going to transform in a blink. What is even better, miracles are always possible; in fact, as more and more people awaken, miracles will become even more likely. *When miracles start to occur, a spiritual tsunami will sweep the planet clean.* But, that is for later. My point here is simply this: even if the tasks ahead seem overwhelming, do not be overwhelmed. Hang in there. Remind yourself, you do not have to do it alone, and help is on the way.

The third thing I want to say about the activation process is this: despite the gargantuan nature of the tasks ahead, you do not have to do it all at once. Feel free to pick little things to start with, especially at the beginning when you may be ignorant of the Truth and inexperienced with the Spirit. In other words, *pick what you can do.* Start with smaller messes first. Clean up those and then move on. Any kind of progress, even turtle-slow, is fine so long as you are making progress.[67] Indeed, even baby steps will get you to your destination in the end. If you have to take baby steps to move forward, do that; and, do not be ashamed about it. We all have different skills and abilities, we all work at different speeds; we all struggle with different things. It doesn't matter how fast or slow you move (unless of course you are dealing with a life or death situation), just so long as you move. Besides, and this is the **fourth thing** I have to say, you will get better, stronger, and faster over time. The more you learn, the more you clean up, the more you properly handle the resistance, the more empowered you become, the easier it will get. Even baby steps involve forward movement! Even a little success can make you feel more empowered. It may be slow at first, but you will get better and faster over time.

To summarize what I have said so far, do not freak out and do not be overwhelmed. You do not have to do it alone, you do not have to do it all at once, even baby steps are progress, and you will get better and stronger over time. That said, you also, and this is the **fifth thing** I want to say, have to be realistic,

---

[67] Unless, of course, you are dealing with a life or death situation, in which case you should muster up as much gumption as you can, get as much help as you can find, and do everything you can to get yourself and others to see the truth, take action, and change, before it is too late.

especially at the beginning. Even though baby steps are fine, even though you will get stronger in the long term, and even though help is on the way, the mess you wake up to may be too much for you to handle. What I mean to say is, you may need to seek competent professional help.[68] Do not be afraid to seek it. If things are really messed up, if your personal space, family space, and life space are extremely toxic, or if you don't know what to do, get help; get help from doctors, get help from psychologists, get help from therapists, get help from empaths, get help from (good) books, get help from guides, etcetera. This is important. There is no shame in asking for help. Do not be afraid to reach out. It is very possible that the help you need is within arm's length already and all you have to do is reach out. So, reach out and ask.

Of course, having said this, I realize there's often not a lot of decent help available, and many people still live in terrible, violent, famine riddled, and war torn situations; here I am really talking to those lucky enough to live in relatively free, relatively developed, relatively non-violent situations. If this is not you, if you live in one of the horrible places that still exist on this Earth, have hope. The current chaos is temporary; the current violence will pass. Things are changing fast and the changes will accelerate over time. Educate yourself; awaken yourself; activate yourself; connect with others around you on the same path; teach others; stand with others; make what changes you can; and, most of all, have patience. Believe me when I say, *it is only a short matter of time before the wave begins to catch up to you.*

---

[68] Speaking of competent and professional help, probably the very last thing you want to do is take advice from friends and family. The situations many of us have to deal with, the messes that lie before us, often require expert guidance and intervention. You would not hand over a complicated modern vehicle for repair to a family or friend if that person had limited or no knowledge of cars. Neither should you trust the advice of people who may have no real psychological, therapeutic, healing, or spiritual knowledge, no matter how close you feel you are to them. If you need help, get it; but be discerning. Not everyone (not even all professionals, really) know what it is they are talking about. *Caveat Emptor,* always.

To summarize: when you get to the point where you realize just how massive the problems are, take a deep breath, calm down, and realize you can do it. Take on chewable chunks, go slow, and ask for help. If you get stuck, hang on. Help is on the way.

Finally, and this is the **sixth and final thing** I want to say about activation, even though you can do it, even though others will follow, and even though it is going to get easier all the time, it is not always going to be a pleasant experience. Stay real. There are all sorts of difficult emotional and psychological challenges ahead. Until (and unless) your whole family, heck, unless the whole world is on board, there will be resistance, blockages, and push back from all those who are too afraid or to blocked up to stand up, wake up, and transform. In situations where there is resistance and blockage, moving forward will be a challenge; but that is OK. I can assure you, it is no longer "business as usual."

Over time, blockages, obstacles, and resistances will transform, dissipate, and finally disappear. It will occur slowly at first, but the transformation, dissipation, and disappearance will accelerate over time. You will know it when you see it.

If this causes you some anxiety and sadness, take a deep breath and relax. Remember, you can do it. You do not have to do it all at once and you get can help if you need it. If you do struggle, remember this: at the very least, while you are healing and fixing things up, protect the children. *If you want to move forward as an individual, if we want to move forward as a planet, it can no longer be business as usual.* From this point on, things have to change.

Ascension

At this point we have discussed in minor detail both awakening and activation. Obviously, this is only the beginning; there is a lot more to say about both. At this time, however, I would like to move on and discuss in a bit more detail the third step on the ladder, which is ascension. The question before us is, "What is ascension?"

I have to admit up front, ascension is one of the oddest things you will encounter on this path. Ascension, at least as defined here, is not something your traditional religions or traditional sciences will have prepared you for. As I explain in a bit more detail in *The Book of Life: Ascension and the Divine World Order*,[69] ascension is about raising the vibration of physical matter and making it easier for Spirit to create. Ascension is exactly like heating up molasses, really. When it is cold, molasses is thick, viscous, and hard to stir. However, when you heat it up, it runs like water. It is the same with physical creation. When it is cold, as it is when the fire of Consciousness is at a distance, it is viscous and thick. However, bring the heat of Consciousness in closer and it runs more like water. This is a big deal because the less viscous physical reality is, the easier it is to change things; and, the easier it is to create/change things, well, the faster it is that things change.

Ascension, like awakening and activation, is a big topic and I cannot really go into any detail here. If you want details on that, see my *Book of Life: Ascension and the Divine World Order*. For now, let me just make it as clear as I can at this stage. Ascension is like applying heat to a bowl of molasses. Ascension is about raising the vibration of physical matter. Ascension, among other things, leads to faster and faster change. Of course, rapid change and transformation is a good thing, especially considering the sorry state of the world. However, rapid change can be challenging, especially if you have done naught to prepare. If you have done nothing to prepare, then your experience of ascension will be a lot like facing repeated fires, tornados, and floods. It will not be pleasant at all. *If you do not want to get knocked on your ass by the spiritual tsunami that is approaching, my advice to you,*

[69] Sharp, The Book of Life: Ascension and the Divine World Order.

my advice to everybody, is this: prepare. If you are not prepared, when the water rises, you risk being knocked flat. Of course, I realize I might be speaking to the choir here since if you are reading these words you are in the process of preparation. Still, it deserves restating. If you want a stable flotation platform upon which to observe the coming changes, prepare, or in your case, continue your preparation work. Do not allow yourself to be sidetracked and do not get bumped off the track.

That is really all I have to say, for now, about awakening, activation, and ascension. In closing, I want to say a few final words. **One**, this excurses on awakening, activation, and ascension is really just an introduction. In this section, I have just set the concepts out and given you a rough overview. An overview is important. The overview gives you the big picture and the big picture helps you see the forest for the trees. However, understanding a few concepts and having the big picture is not sufficient. Even though you have an overview, many of the details are missing; and I have to say, details are important. Indeed, transformation is in the details. So, from this point on we are going to fill in all the necessary details. We will fill in the cosmological details; we will fill in the psychological details; we will fill in the healing details; we will fill in transformational details, etc. We cannot do that overnight; there is some reading and work involved; and, if you want to make progress, you need to buckle down, pay attention, and work. Nevertheless, have faith; we will do it.

The **second thing** I want to say is this. Awakening, activation, and ascension is not a linear process. That is, it does not occur on a straight line. This is an iterative spiral process that moves back and forth in a complex cosmic dance of Consciousness and creation. You awaken a little (or a lot); you activate a little (or a lot); you and your environment ascends a little (or a lot), as the individual case may be. As such, there is no particular right or wrong way to do it. In this regard, in all regards really,

Spirit/higher Self/God is pragmatic. Follow your intuition/interest! Work on what you are anxious to work on. Work on what you want to work on. Once you step onto the path, everything guides your way.

Besides an admonishment that this is just an introduction and a heads up that this is not a linear process, the **third thing** I want to say is this: this does not just happen and then you are done. That is, this is not a magical process that instantly transforms you. Well, that is not quite true. As my own biography and the biography of many others reveals, instant transformation is possible. Even so, real work is involved. There is real work and it takes real time. You have to process, integrate, and ground. It does not happen overnight; it does not happen in a crystal instant; and it certainly does not happen dressed in silly robes and performing impotent rituals. If you think any of these things, you are deluding yourself. I have said it before and I will say it again until I am sure the whole world has heard; the process is challenging and it takes work. So buckle down and get to work.

The Importance of Breathing

In the last section of this workbook, we talked a bit about the nature of awakening, activation, and ascension. There I tried to give you a big picture sense of what each are about. Before that, I also gave you some practical advice on kick starting the process itself. The basic advice I provided was simple. Get yourself aligned and set your intent. As I noted earlier, and as explained in detail in *Lightning Path Workbook One: Introduction to the Lightning Path,* the goal of the process is to make a connection, however brief, to Consciousness.

I suppose the question at this point is what happens when you do connect to Consciousness? What happens when you connect to The Fabric? What happens when you link up with the brightest Light in the universe, your higher Self? That is a good question, and a big question, and unfortunately, I cannot go into a lot of detail here. The problem is, many different things could happen. You could experience grand revelations of cosmic identity and a total revolution of purpose; or, in rare cases, you might experience semi-permanent (or even permanent) psychosis. You can have little "nature experiences," moderate peak experiences, or massive transcendent experiences. You could talk to God, talk to your higher Self, or even communicate better with your cat. What the experience is and what it is like depends on many different things. It is impossible to predict in advance, and it is impossible to discuss in this short introductory document. Putting that discussion aside for now, in this chapter I want to talk a bit about breathing.

Now, I have said it before and I will say it again, *when connecting to Consciousness, breathing is important.*[70] Connecting to consciousness can be a very challenging process.

---

[70] An alternative discussion of the significance and important of breathing may be found in my book *The Great Awakening: Concepts and Techniques for Successful Spiritual Practice.*

It can challenge you intellectually, morally, psychologically, and emotionally. The truth is, when you connect and awaken, even if only for a few moments or so, you are shining a bright light on yourself, your families, and the realities of this world, and what you see can suck very badly. And I'm not just talking about the suckiness of global poverty, violence, and war; I'm talking about the suckiness of violent, desperate, and empty lives, filled with despair and hopelessness, and prowled about by predators, pedophiles, and the like. If you have not already seen it around you, you certainly will as you become more connected. On Earth, all the awesome beauty and grandeur of this creation is often submerged behind an ugly world and an often ugly and twisted life space. That is a problem because when you confront the truths of this world, or your life, or your behaviors, emotions can run high, fears can bubble up, and confusion can strangle you cold. From the political and economic truths of this world to your own victimization, complicity and guilt, the first few moments of a **Connection Experience**[71] can feel like being hit with a category five tornado; there is shock, struggle, and awe. It is not always like this of course. You can, and will, have beautiful, warm and fuzzy connection experiences, what I call **Zenith Experiences**,[72] where you feel one with nature, the universe, and even God. But, and this is important, you can also have negative, **Nadir Experiences**.[73] Nadir experiences are negative connection experiences characterized by confusion, anxiety, guilt, shame, and even (if you are with the wrong people) psychic and spiritual assault.

---

[71] A connection experience (a.k.a. Connection Event) is the LP term for mystical experience, mystical connection, union with God, etc. http://www.thespiritwiki.com/Connection_Experience.

[72] A Zenith Experience is any positively felt connection experience. A zenith experience may range in power from minor nature and peak experiences through to full blown visionary revelation. http://www.thespiritwiki.com/Zenith_Experience.

[73] http://www.thespiritwiki.com/Nadir_Experience.

If you have a zenith experience, then the biggest challenge is integrating and grounding the information without blowing off the top of your skull. Unless there is serious damage to your bodily ego, everything is usually hunky dory, even after intense zenith awakening; to be sure, sometimes it can take a few days to get over the blast, but you usually do. On the other hand, nadir experiences can be more challenging. The question here is, what do you do if you have a nadir experience? What do you do if, in your awakening process, you get dumped into fear, confusion, paranoia, and other "dark night of the soul" stuff? Really, the best, and often the only thing you can do if that happens to you, is deep breathe. Whenever you get blasted by a nadir experience, whenever you are overwhelmed by the storm, whenever you are hit with fear, confusion or other powerful emotions, you need to breathe. When it comes to handling the emotional and psychological sequelae of connection experiences, remembering to deep breathe is important.

Why?

Because *deep breathing is an important spiritual practice with deep cosmological roots.* As I note in *The Book of Light: The Nature of God, the Structure of Consciousness, and the Universe Within You,* breath is literally the fuel of creation. Not only that, it is the fuel of your physical body and mind. If you do not breathe, you die within minutes. More to the point, if you do not breathe, you cut off your body's supply of oxygen. Without adequate oxygen, your body and (more importantly here) your mind do not function at optimum levels; and the deterioration is quick. If we stop breathing, as we often do in times of intensity and crises, it can take only seconds for you to collapse. Remember this. It is hard enough to deal with the emotional and psychological storm that sometimes accompanies nadir experiences; if you hold your breath you are depriving your body of the fuel it needs to cope and survive.

It is important you keep this in mind.

Deep breathing helps your body function properly, and proper function is needed in times of great stress.[74] Deep breathing slows your heart, oxygenates your brain, returns blood from the extremities, and reduces adrenalin in the bloodstream. *Deep breathing calms you and helps you focus.* It might sound ridiculously trivial to some, but deep breathing is critical and can make the difference between overwhelming fear, panic and anxiety, and calm, grounded, and empowered forward movement. Of course, breathing is not a miracle cure. Breathing is not the only thing that you have to do to keep moving forward; however, it is part of a backpack of tools that you should have with you on your journey home. When you are feeling anxious, afraid, stressed, shocked or otherwise discombobulated by the things you are feeling and seeing, the first thing you need to do (assuming you are not dealing with immediate threats to your physical survival) is take deep breaths.

Thankfully, as long as you maintain a certain assemblage of your wits, that is easy. To breathe properly, sit up straight, straighten your spine, raise your chin so your head is straight, close your eyes, and breathe in, breathe out. Breathe in; breathe out. You can even add a visualization to make it work better if you like. For example, when I am trying to calm down, I like to visualize a leaf gently falling from a tree. This is just one example. You can use any calming visualization to go along with your deep breathing that you want.

Just breathe in, breathe out.

Breathe in; breathe out.

Do it at least three times and more if you need to. Moreover, note, you do not necessarily have to "assume the position" (i.e. back straight, head straight, spine straight, lotus position, etc.) to get benefits from deep breathing. If you are hunched over in

---

[74] For an overview of the body's stress response, see Anonymous, "Understanding the Stress Response," <u>Harvard Health Publications</u> 2016. http://www.health.harvard.edu/staying-healthy/understanding-the-stress-response/.

a state of great anxiety or fear and all you can manage is deep gasps, that is fine too, so long as you eventually straighten up. Of course, you should aim for the more technically correct practice whenever you can, even when you are breathing for creative and not anxiety management purposes; but in an emotionally charged pinch, any deep breathing will help. It sounds basic I know, but do not let that fool you. It works like a charm.

At this point, I have spoken a bit about the challenges and pitfalls of awakening. I have even suggested that you might have to look forward to nadir experiences and I have said that in order to prepare for those you need, amongst other things, to learn to breathe properly. At this point, your anxiety levels may be rising a bit and if so, pause and take a deep breath. It is a challenge that is for sure, but it is not random, and you do have control. Also, believe me when I tell you, you do not have to deal with everything that comes up as it comes up, or all at once, or by yourself. Pick your battles (do the easier ones first), take your time, and get help when you need it. Moreover, *the hardest part is in the early stages*. In the early stages when indoctrination has its strongest hold, when the room is a total mess, and when ignorance of truth and denial of reality are high, it can be tough. However, that changes very quickly. Once you begin to face the truth, clean the mess, and remove obstacles, things can change very quickly.

Just how quickly can things change? If my case is any indication, it can change overnight. For myself, I spent my first 39 years in indoctrinated disconnection. Except for a few preemptive connection experiences when I was a young adult, I walked around totally disconnected for over 30 years. Of course, we all have different reasons for our disconnection. My problem was primarily my Catholic indoctrination. To make a long story short, the lies that the priests told had seeded deep fears in me. Whenever I came close to real connection, these fears caused me to shut it down. The problem was, the Catholic Church had made me afraid of "the other side." When this fear was invoked, I turned tail and fled (i.e. I shut the connection down and gave up on authentic spiritual practice). Of course, I did not walk around in constant terror and confusion of God. In fact, while walking around in normal consciousness I was not even aware I had this fear. However, strong connection triggered the fear and the connection shut down.

However, as I said, this can change fast. In fact, for me it changed overnight.[75] One night I cleared the fear and it was done. After that, things moved quickly indeed. I learned about the chains that had been placed on my mind, I learned to see and face reality, I learned about all the damage that had been done, *I learned to control my fear and my thoughts*, and I learned to ground and control. We are looking at a time span of six months, maybe a year. Through all that, I relied on deep breathing to center and ground. So, remember to breathe. As the Light begins to shine and the facade begins to crumble, remember to breathe. Breathing, and some other practices which we will discuss as we progress, is what will get you through.

Before moving on to our next topic of discussion, two final things. **One**, and at the risk of beating an already dead horse, if you need help, ask for it. Despite what some might impute, there is no shame in showing "weakness" or getting help. If you need help straightening things out, if you are overwhelmed by what you see, if you are incapable of dealing with the old world nonsense that surrounds you – like for example the presence of a pedophile in your family, or the emotional fallout of childhood abuse – ask for help. Only a fool stands alone in the middle of a burning house with only a wish and a prayer. If you

---

[75] For a more complete recounting of the "overnight" transformation, see Michael Sharp, Lightning Path Workbook Two - Introduction to the Lightning Path, Lightning Path Workbook Series, St. Albert, Alberta. A brief recounting is also provided in Mike Sosteric, "Mysticism, Consciousness, Death," Journal of Consciousness Exploration and Research 7.11 (2016).

need help, get help.

Second, and finally, I should say that awakening and activation will involve more than just psychological and emotional turmoil, so do not think I am the bringer of sorrow and bad tidings. Quite the opposite is true, in fact. Awakening and activation will also involve energetic expansion, feelings of love, bliss, awareness, connection, glorious realizations of your divinity (and the divinity of others), intuitive unfoldings, incredible feelings of empowerment, and all sorts of positive and wonderful zenith experiences. Just remember, getting to those experiences, and having them without overtones of fear, anxiety, guilt and even paranoia, means first facing down the state of the room you are in, clearing blockages, and cleaning up. It is the only way forward. Take a deep breath and get moving.

Staying the Course

In the last chapter we talked a bit about the importance of breathing and some of the fears and issues it can help you with. We learned, among other things, that breathing is an important stress, anxiety, and panic management tool. It may have been a bit of a surprise to consider the spiritual awakening process as a potentially difficult and challenging one, especially since these days so much spiritual fluff emphasizes unquestioning faith, unfettered consumerism, and "positive" ignorance as spiritual practices, but it can be. In the context of authentic spiritual awakening and the challenges that you may sometimes face, intent and breathing are critical tools to help keep you focused and pointed on the straight and narrow.

Moving forward, I want to take a few pages to talk about what happens if, despite all your good intentions to the contrary, you are delayed and/or bumped off the Path. Unfortunately, it is a definite possibility! One minute you can be making good progress towards connection, maybe even having some powerful connection experiences, and the next you can be distracted, turned away, or halted dead in your tracks. It happens all the time. If that happens to you, what do you do?

First, if it does happen, you have to distinguish between a time out/rest period and actually getting bumped off the path. Both can happen. You may not like to hear this, especially if you have been into those "law of attraction" style spiritualties where the goal is simply to get wealthy, but that is the truth. The Lightning Path, indeed any authentic spiritual path, is not about attraction, individual prosperity, reward in the after-life, and acceptance of what is; it is about awakening to horrible , and of course beautiful, realities, the elimination of individual and global disjuncture, the reconnection of the masses, and transformation of the planet. This is a major challenge at both an individual and a collective level, especially when you also consider the fact that awakening, activation, removal of obstacles, and forward movement involves sweeping away the crumbling old world.[76] It can be hard to do. It can even be shocking and overwhelming, which is fine. If you become so shocked by the scope of the work that you cannot move forward, if you are so overwhelmed by the enormity of it all that you need to take a break and/or stick your head back in the sand for a while, if you get spun around in confusion, experience frustration and anxiety and decide you need to take some time off to process, that's OK. That happens. If you need to fugue a little while and let others carry the weight, that is fine. There is nothing particularly wrong with wending a circuitous route toward final awakening and activation. We all have different life circumstances; we all have difficult decisions to make; we are all more or less responsible for others; we all have unique issues and struggles to deal with. Ergo, we all need to go at a different pace and follow a slightly different course. This is not a big deal. There is no one–size-fits-all solution. You do not have to follow a timed and graded path through it all and you certainly do not have to feel bad if you need to move a little slower. My advice to you is, take your time! Rest, relax, process the information, learn what you need to learn, strengthen in those areas you need to strengthen, and move forward at a pace and with a purpose with which you are comfortable.

Trust your gut and follow your own feelings on this. Are you feeling a little overwhelmed, frightened, or discombobulated? Is fear overwhelming you and threatening to snap the fragile mental stability of your physical unit? Are you exhausted and confused by the information that you have to process? Then, take a break for a short time. Step off the path, Netflix, chill, and go on a little spiritual hiatus. This is not a race. Slow and

---

[76] Sweeping away the old is a necessary, at times difficult, and sometimes even sad chore ahead. Unfortunately, you do not have a choice in this. You cannot build a new building on top of a crumbling old one. Neither can you build a new utopian reality on the top of the debris and detritus of our current dystopia. No matter how you try to fit the two together, it will just not work. You either stick wholly with the old, or clear that away and embrace thoroughly the new.

steady gets you there just the same.

And remember, this goes both ways here. Listen to your feelings to tell you when you need to slow down or pause, but also listen to them when they tell you it is time to get moving. Are you feeling anxious and unsettled, like you should be doing something? Is there a strong internal drive pushing you in a forward direction? Are you impatient with aspects of your life or the people in it? Are you having a hard time denying the truth? Then, get back to it. Trust your gut, move forward with purpose, and make the changes you need. Do not be unnecessarily negative about things; but, always remember, do not stay stuck too long. The general message I have for you here is simple: chill out. Relax, calm down, go slow, and take a break if you need to. Everybody walking an authentic spiritual path will need to do this at one time or another. It is not a big deal. Just remember to start moving again when you are ready.

As noted above, there are two reasons that can stall you on your authentic path. One is because you are taking a break and the other is because, through no intent of your own, you get bumped off the path. This can happen easily, especially considering how many distractions and diversions are intentionally thrown in your way. Given all the sparkly crap thrown on the road, it is very easy to get stalled in your tracks or even led quietly astray. Despite the fact that the drive to spiritually awaken is hard-coded in your genetic DNA, and despite the fact that the drive is strong, it happens ongoing to billions! It will happen less as time passes, but it still does happen, it will continue to happen, and it may (perhaps already has) even happened to you. One day you are reading, practicing the mantras, and moving forward, and the next day you have forgotten it all and moved back to "normal" life. One moment you are dancing in the sunrise of Spirit, the next you have fallen and are eclipsed by the delusions of The System. It happens to me. It happens to everybody. It is not a problem so long as you snap out real quick.

The question is, "How do you tell?" How do you tell if your dancing in the rising sun or sleeping by the light of the moon? How do you tell if you are moving forward in the light of the spirit or stuck in the darkness of ego? That is easy. **First of all**, scan your life-space for violence of any form. Violence of any kind is a sure sign you are stuck. The bottom line is, there should be no violence in your life. This is a basic starter requirement and it is a sure sign of forward movement, or lack thereof. If there is violence in your life, you cannot just ignore it and let it be. Violence of any kind will throw you off the path faster than you can say boo. To repeat, *you cannot move forward on an authentic spiritual path when you are surrounded by constant violence and aggression.* It just does not work that way. The two are mutually incompatible. In an ideal life space, one that allows you to function properly, live, and grow in power and divinity, there should be absolutely zero-zip-nada violence.[77]

If you look around and you do find violence in your life, what do you do? If you are truly interested in moving forward, you do whatever you need to do to end the violence. The reality is, you cannot move forward on the Path while you are subject to, or engaging in, assault, violence, and exploitation. It just does not work that way. You might make some progress, but the violence will generally interfere because it will keep you distracted and focused on defense. It will corrupt your

---

[77] Of course, there is a bit of a quandary here. A no violence rule is all very fine and dandy on a world where everybody is wide-awake, empowered, connected and respectful of boundaries. On a world like that, there is going to be no war, violence, adultery, deception, and theft from the poor. On a world like that, simply raising your hands would be enough to get people to stop. Unfortunately, we do not have that world, yet. Soon, but not yet. On this world, people run roughshod over boundaries all the time. Worse than that, on this world people intentionally exploit each other on a minute-to-minute basis. And note, it is not just the rich who do this. Our employers, our governments, our sisters, our brothers, and even our moms and our dads hurt, hit, steal, and exploit us. What is worse, when you tell them to stop, they often do not. In fact, when you tell the people of this world to stop, they often redouble their efforts out of pure spite. It is ridiculous that it happens, but it does. Even so, even though it is challenging, you must strive for nonviolence.

understanding and interpretation of what you are reading. It will damage your body (if it is physical violence) and mind (if it is psychological or emotional violence). In the end, the disjuncture caused by it will undermine your ability to connect and stay connected. So do what you need to do to a) stop your own acts and b) keep violent actors away. It is very important. If you want to stay focused on the path, if you want to make consistent forward progress, you need to achieve a calm and safe environment as quickly and as completely as you can.[78] This is very important. If you want to move forward, if we all want to move forward, the violence must end <u>now</u>.

If you are getting a little verklempt right now, relax. I know that given the current state of the planet, saying that we need to stop the violence immediately seems hopelessly utopian. Perhaps, but regardless, you can still start. Start with yourself because that is the easiest. Just stop being violent. Stop shooting others, stop hitting your children, stop screaming and yelling, stop being angry, stop passive aggressive emotional attacks, stop exploiting people, stop hurting others, just, stop, stop, stop. Set an example and stop. It might take a while, but you can do it and when you do, when you have made a little progress on yourself, get to work on your family. Teach your spouse and your children non-violence. Discuss with them the importance of calm, safe spaces for emotional, psychological, and spiritual development. Then, when you have established the foundation in your family, start on your work or professional environment. Finally, work in the political and economic spheres.[79] I know it

---

[78] Visualizations can help in this regard. To keep violence out of your life, use, for example, **boundary visualization.** Boundary visualizations are simply visualizations that help you establish and reinforce personal safe zones. I provide one or two in my book *The Great Awakening: Concepts and Techniques for Successful Spiritual Practice,* but they are easy to imagine for yourself. Just visualize balloons, brick walls, energetic barriers, or whatever you like really, keeping you safe from the maelstrom. Note, if visualization does not work to keep negative people away, if for example they break through your boundaries no matter what you do, or if you find yourself unable to establish and maintain boundaries, seek professional assistance.

[79] For those of you studying to be LP mentors/therapists, we look at this widening area of work in terms of **Spheres**

is a lot of work, and I know there is a lot of resistance now, but you will be surprised at just how fast resistance will start to drop away and transformation will unfold once you make a decision and focus. It will start slow at first, but it will accelerate quickly. It is going to be frightening at times, but take a deep breath. Remember, *it is good that the resistance dissipates.* Keep telling yourself, "We are moving towards a better world for everybody," keep pushing in a transformative direction, and before you know it you will be telling yourself that you will never go back to "that" toxicity again.

As noted, if you find yourself bumped off the path, the first thing you look for is violence. The **second cause and symptom** of "spiritual interruptus" is misplaced priorities. The truth is, *if you want to move forward on a spiritual path, you need to establish priorities, and one of your priorities has to be spiritual awakening.* Why? Because, you, and when I say "you" here I really mean your physical body and little bodily ego, have a limited amount of energy to expend in a day. You start the day with the cup full, but the energy drains throughout the day. By end of day, your energy is depleted. When your energy is depleted, you go to sleep to regenerate and replenish. You start each new day with a new pool of energy, but watch out; you do not have an unlimited reserve nor do you have unlimited time. You only have so much time and energy to expend throughout the day. When you run out of time and have used up your energy, you are done and you will fall asleep exhausted.[80] It is important to keep this in mind, particularly since the process of awakening and activation takes a lot of time and energy. If you

---

of Alignment. We help our clients align themselves in widening spheres of influence. First, we start them in the individual sphere, then we get them to work on their family and social situations, finally we encourage them to get active in transformation at work, in government, and so on. The individual's life transforms as they increasingly align (with Consciousness) in the widening spheres of influence. For a more detailed treatment, see www.thespiritwiki.com/Spheres_of_Alignment/.

[80] Of course, you can push the energy limits of your body with drugs, but this will damage your body and mind in ways that we have not even begun to understand.

do not give it the time it needs, if you find yourself too busy doing other things so you have no time to read an LP book, study some LP concepts, and practice some LP visualizations, you are not moving forward. It is as simple as that. If you are finding that you are not devoting any time or energy to your spiritual training and advancement, you will need to set some priorities and cut some things out of your life so that you have the time and energy to accomplish this most important goal. That is all there is to it. Examine the time and energy you devote to spiritual study and practice. If you are not devoting much, or any, straighten out your priorities so you can get back on track. It is not going to happen if you do not do the work.

So far I have noted that if you are concerned to stay on track you need to look at violence in your life and you need to examine priorities to make sure you have the time and energy you need. **The third thing** that you want to watch for is, to be blunt, spiritual crap. That is, keep a good watch on the materials that you are using, the advice you are accepting, the books you are reading, and the shows you are watching. If you find you are being bumped off the path, if you sense you are getting stuck, if it feels like you are spinning around in circles a little too much, take a look at what you are reading, watching, and listening to. You may not have ever thought about it, but the truth is, there is a lot of spiritual crap out there, and it is not at all harmless! Some of the spiritual crap can hurt you: some can even get you killed.[81] The truth is, not all spiritual materials, or spiritual authors for that matter, are worth it. Some spiritual materials are poorly written, some are ideological in nature, and some are just plain wrong. Similarly, some spiritual authors cannot write, some spew nothing but "pain body" ideology, and some know absolutely nothing at all about what they are talking about. Some have never had a spiritual/connection experience at all while others have a single spiritual experience or two and then

---

[81] Just think about "spiritual" teachers that encourage you to strap bombs to your body and blow yourself up.

sell themselves off like experts in the field. Some spiritual authors are even mentally ill! I do not want to go into detail here, nor do I feel comfortable naming names,[82] but you have to be aware of these issues, you have to pay attention to what you are putting into your mind, and you have to learn to discern the spiritual wheat from the useless chaff.[83] If you do not, you could end up wasting your whole life following somebody else's confusion, pathology, or ideological special interest. Since I do not recommend you waste your life, *pay attention* and be critical. If you find you are not making any progress, consider the materials you are reading. If you get the sense that something might be off, trust your gut and move on.

And that is all I have to say about that. In this chapter, I have examined the importance of staying the course and staying on path. I have also examined some of the reasons why you might not stay the course. As we have seen, sometimes we can take breaks, and sometimes we can be distracted or bumped off the path. It is fine if you take breaks. Just remember to get moving again. As for being bumped off the path, my basic advice to you is pay attention. If you find you are not making as much progress as you like, look for violence, distraction, manipulation, and just plain spiritual incompetence. Also, examine your priorities. It does not matter how rich and powerful you are, you only have so much energy and time in a day. *If you waste time and energy on materialist pursuits, bullshit ideology, or incompetent gurus, you will not make any spiritual progress.* If you are serious about spiritual awakening, you have to stay on path. If you do not stay on Path, you will go down with the sinking old energy ship. Take this to heart and put it into practice. Stay focused, devoted, and on Path.

---

[82] Though, in the interest of the millions who are spiritually betrayed, spiritual talk-show hucksters and the charlatans they endorse really need to be called out.

[83] I got some ideas about how to discern the wheat from the chaff. See Sharp, The Rocket Scientists' Guide to Spiritual Discernment.

Boundaries Redux

In the last few lessons, we have talked about breathing, intent, awakening/activation challenges, and the importance of staying the course. These are all important discussions and they can help you stay focused and moving forward as you struggle through the mess and the confusion that surrounds you. As I said at the end of the last chapter, take this information to heart and put it into practice. It is designed to provide a foundation for consistent and persistent forward movement. Speaking of forward movement, I also want to remind you, because it is very important, this is not a race. *The goal is not to get to the finish line first; the goal is to make constant forward progress at a pace that you find reasonable and comfortable,* and at a rate that will not traumatize you to the point where you disappear from your path of spiritual awakening altogether.

In this chapter, I want to revisit another thing that can help you stay focused and on point and that thing is boundaries. I have talked about boundaries elsewhere,[84] but the material is important and worth repeating. The truth is, *if you are serious about awakening and empowerment, if you are going to succeed in your awakening and activation efforts, you are going to have to get some boundaries.* Boundaries are important for spiritual progress for several reasons.

- Boundaries help you create safe spaces.

- Boundaries help you wrestle free time and energy from your oversaturated life.

- Boundaries help ensure your emotional and psychological needs are completely satisfied.

- Finally, boundaries help ensure you are healthy and

---

[84] I speak about boundaries in Michael Sharp, <u>Lightning Path Workbook One - Introduction to Authentic Spirituality</u>, Lightning Path Workbook Series, vol. 1 (St. Albert, Alberta: Lightning Path Press, 2016). Also Sharp, <u>The Great Awakening: Concepts and Techniques for Successful Spiritual Practice</u>.

whole.

All these things are necessary and will help you make good forward progress. Perhaps it sounds a bit trite to say it here, but you cannot run out of a burning house, you cannot put out a fire, you cannot eat a simple meal, and you certainly cannot make spiritual progress forward while you are the subject of constant boundary violations (i.e. physical, psychological, emotional, and even spiritual assault). It is just not possible. It does not make sense from a gross physical perspective (how can you do anything while somebody is constantly assaulting you), it does not make mental or emotional sense, and it certainly does not make sense from a spiritual perspective. In fact, it is a particular problem when you are trying to make spiritual progress forward. If you want to succeed in this regard, you have to make sure that everything is arranged right and correct. It will not happen otherwise, not only because you push and Consciousness pulls away when things are not right, but also because bringing Consciousness into the body is the hardest thing you will ever do.

It is true. **Consciousness is all things**. Consciousness is vast. Consciousness is expansive. Getting even a little bit of that higher consciousness into your body can be a challenge, particularly after enduring a toxic socialization process. Getting the full power and glory into your body full time is a major undertaking. In this context, a healthy mind and healthy emotions[85] are essential prerequisites of spiritual advancement. The bottom line is, you will not be able to contain consciousness in your physical unit (your body/mind) unless you are healthy, whole, and free of ongoing assault.

---

[85] Physical health is important as well, but physical disabilities and physical injuries do not prevent consciousness from entering the physical unit. A broken arm, a broken back, heart disease, these are not things that affect the descent of consciousness. However, if these things arise from toxic life environments, if a broken arm is the result of spousal abuse, that is a different story. If the underlying cause of physical illness and disability is toxicity in the life space, the toxicity in the life space will have an impact.

This is very important, so I will repeat. *An undamaged and healthy physical unit is a basic requirement of spiritual awakening and activation.*[86] Therefore, if you want to make spiritual progress, if you want to awaken and empower, one of the first things you have to do is stop the abuse. You have no choice. Either you stop it, or you do not make progress. And here's the kicker: when it comes to spiritual awakening and empowerment, asserting boundaries becomes more important the more awake you are. The more awake you are, the more Consciousness you have in the body, the more sensitive you become. Putting this another way, the more aware you are, the more lack of boundaries is going to hurt you. When you are aware of the functioning of your body, when you are aware of the pain that assault causes, when you feel the damage as it spreads out through your physical, mental, and emotional being, when you are not repressing, i.e. when you are aware, you bear the full brunt of any assaults that occur.[87] Believe me when I say, spiritual awakening and empowerment without attention to boundaries is a recipe for pain, suffering, and psychological/emotional disaster. If you want to make spiritual progress forward, you need to establish boundaries.

If you are moving forward, I should not have to convince you of any of this. As Consciousness descends, you are going to become more aware of past damage, past assault, and current

---

[86] Be careful and sensible here. A broken bone, some torn cartilage, heart conditions, and so on don't stop consciousness from descending, but the drugs you take to manage the pain might. Similarly, a toxic blowout here and there is not going to impede your awakening, but indoctrination as a child, unmet psychological meets, and damage to your bodily ego and self-esteem will. Also keep in mind, you can heal bodily and mental damage. If you feel there is damage, investigate and make healing that damage a priority. Still, healthy body and mind are important so my advice to you is, get some boundaries and stop the violence and assault.

[87] Note, even if you are not aware, you are still being damaged by the assault, you just do not feel it as much. You numb yourself through your lack of awareness. This is a bit of a problem because while unaware you may think you can handle the assaults, but you cannot. Like a boxer whose job is to put themselves on abusive display, you can desensitize yourself to the blows, block awareness of the damage, and use drugs and alcohol to cope. However, as the fifty-year-old boxer often painfully realizes, even when you are not aware, damage accrues.

pain and attack. You are going to see it, feel it, become increasingly aware of the consequences, and increasingly sensitive to ongoing damage. Thus, you need to be aware of the importance of boundaries and you need to do something to get some.

It should be straightforward. The problem is, it is not. Even when we see the violence and toxicity, and even when we feel the damage, we often do not do a darn thing about it! We see the damage and feel the assault, yet we stand impotent as lambs waiting for slaughter. We do not create the boundaries that we need to create; we do not remove ourselves from abusive situations even when we are physically able to do so; we do not tell people to step off and desist. We expose ourselves to violence and abuse even when we know that we should not. The question before us now is, "Why do we fail to create boundaries even when we know that it is something we need to do?" Unfortunately, this is not a straightforward question to answer. There are many reasons why we fail to create boundaries. Some of the reasons are rooted in our own childhood abuse. Some are rooted in guilt and shame over the actions that we ourselves have committed. Some are rooted in the angst and anxiety manifest in our bodies. Sorting it all out it can be a complex spiritual/therapeutic task, but I can say a couple of things here to help get you moving in the right direction.

First off, think right thoughts and not wrong thoughts. Right thoughts are important. Right thoughts can make the difference between failing to assert boundaries and getting the heck out of a toxic situation. Right thought can make the difference between a lifetime of abuse and a life lived on an island of tranquil safety. Allow me to illustrate. Ideas we have in our head often discourage us from having boundaries. Sounds perverse I know, but people often associate being "boundary less" with being a good, even spiritual, person. Jesus Christ said, or so we are told, "Turn the other cheek." Fake priests, false gurus, and "talk show" rishis often admonish us to forgive, forget, find the silver lining, learn from our lessons, ignore our "pain bodies," and just let go. It is true. Billions of people on this planet believe that we should accept misfortune, violence, and abuse because it provides some valuable cosmic lesson, because it somehow demonstrates our moral superiority, because it is part of our "karmic debt," or because they think that "what doesn't kill you makes you stronger."

And look...

Do not get me wrong here...

There is nothing wrong with turning the other cheek, moving on, and letting go. In fact, I recommend that. You are not living a spiritual life if you violently lash out at others just because they hurt you; but, you have to understand, turning the other cheek and letting things go is not the same as having no boundaries. You can turn the other cheek at the same time as you say, "stay away from me and my children." You can forgive the violence of a perpetrator while also determining that you will never be in the same room with that person again. You can set your intent to forgive even while you go to the police for help to stop your abusive wife or husband from hurting you anymore. By all means, forgive and forget; but, maintain your boundaries. Do not sacrifice yourself, your children, or your family because of some misplaced spiritual notions. It is not worth it, and it is incompatible with authentic spirituality. I have seen people with one (or all) of the above misconceptions in place put up with incredible levels of abuse, to the detriment of their long (and even short) term health and survival, and the health of their children. They do so because they consciously or unconsciously believe that doing so makes them a good person, or because they believe the abuse might actually be good for them, or because it is God's plan. However, none of this is true. If you want to make forward progress, if you want to heal, if you want to awaken, the first thing you have to do is disabuse yourself of ideas that discourage boundaries. Turning the other cheek is OK. Forgiving others is OK. However, do not stand there and expose yourself to constant assault and abuse. Get out, get away, and build boundaries.

As you can see, wrong ideas (a.k.a. wrong thought) about karma, forgiveness, and what it means to be a spiritual person can discourage us from creating and maintaining boundaries.[88] Wrong ideas are not the only thing that can prevent boundaries. Bad experience can also teach us to avoid boundaries. This is complicated, and a little perverse, so pay attention. Many of us learn, from hard personal experience, that boundaries are not respected, allowed, or even exist. This is a lesson that many of us learn as children, particularly when our parents and teachers abuse us. Every time a parent hits, hurts, screams at, insults, injures, or intentionally harms a child, the child's nascent ability to build boundaries is undermined. If the abuse goes on long enough and is severe enough, the child's ability to build and maintain boundaries can be destroyed.

Why?

Because as children we are psychologically, emotionally, spiritually, and physically weaker than every single teenager and adult around us. As a consequence of our underdevelopment and weakness, we do not know about nor do we have the strength to enforce our own boundaries. Because we are small and weak, we are completely dependent on the adults around us not only to teach us about the importance of boundaries, but also to respect our boundaries. If they choose not to, if they do not teach the importance of boundaries or worse, if our parents, friends, teachers, and police officers beat, damage, and otherwise hurt us because they are neither aware of nor respect our boundaries, we never learn we can have boundaries and we never learn to build them or maintain them. The truth is, we

---

[88] I know I have said this in previous LP workbooks, and at the risk of beating a dead horse, I go into great depth and detail about right and wrong thought in the LP *Book of the Triumph of Spirit* series. For more details, see http://www.thespiritwiki.com/Book_of_the_Triumph_of_Spirit/.

live in a world of people who know nothing about boundaries and who have no problem violating them any time they feel like. We teach our children to live in a boundary less world and we grow up damaged and psychologically defenseless as a result. It is a massive global oversight in the way we raise our children, and it has to stop, NOW.

Listen to me, because the next thing I say is critical. If you are serious about transforming yourself and your life, open your eyes to your actions and stop hurting the children. Realize, human children are one of the weakest, most vulnerable and most sensitive forms of life on this planet. They need boundaries to survive, grow, and thrive. If you do not teach them about boundaries, or worse if you violate their boundaries just because you can, they will struggle with Consciousness, and so will you. Get it through your head; boundaries are important.

I have many examples from my own childhood and my therapeutic practice of adults failing to teach their children about boundaries, failing to protect their weak children from the assault of others, and even blasting through the boundaries of their own children. My own mother, trained in the Catholic "spare the rod, spoil the child" school of parenting, never said a single thing about boundaries, was never concerned that I should have them, and would regularly violate them with physical and emotional violence. She would hit me with wooden spoons and belts, and would hit even harder, and scream louder, when I begged and pleaded that she stop. I also remember the emotional and psychological abuse of teachers who never thought twice about using ridicule and shame to control and assault. As a child I protested these abuses; but because the adults in my life were more powerful than me, because they had no respect for any boundaries that I tried to assert, and because they ignored me and even redoubled their assault whenever I protested, I learned that boundaries didn't exist. Like the dogs in the original learned helplessness experiments,[89] I learned a boundary less world. Though you would never know it if looked at me then, it impacted me profoundly. The hurt and the pain (not to mention the BS and the ideology) that I allowed in because of my lack of boundaries built up damage over the years that made my awakening process, and in particular early initiatory events, challenging. It took longer than it needed to take and it was harder than it needed to be. What's more, there was a small chance I might fail. There was a small possibility that I could have been permanently hobbled and my mission and plan thrown completely off track to the point where I died while still asleep, which would have been a shame.

And, do not get me wrong here. It is the same for you. The failure of your parents to teach you about boundaries, coupled with the adult failure to respect boundaries, and your consequent lack of awareness about the importance of boundaries, is not a good thing. It hurts you, damages you, potentially pre-empts your awakening, and prevents you from fulfilling your mission. So, stop. Stop violating the boundaries of others (especially small children) and stop letting others violate yours, for any reason. Despite what you have been told, there are no good reasons to put up with abuse. In fact, as scientists are increasingly seeing, violence and abuse of any form damages.[90] The bottom line is, if you want to make spiritual progress, heck if you want to live a good life, you got to protect yourself from harm. As I have repeatedly stated, assault damages the body and mind. If you expose yourself to assault, you will be unable to make spiritual progress. Therefore, there is only one thing to do and that is, get some boundaries.

I will talk in more detail about the importance of boundaries and some of the obstacles you might face in developing them

---

[89] See https://en.wikipedia.org/wiki/Learned_helplessness/.

[90] For a quick and dirty run down of the damage, see my article Sosteric, "Toxic Socialization."

in Lightning Path Workbook Four. For now, I just want to get you started by giving you one initial piece of advice on how to build boundaries. The advice is simply this: ask for them. Start building your boundaries by telling those around you what they are and asking, nay demanding, that they respect them. Whether they are hurting you physically, emotionally, psychologically, or spiritually, whether they are laughing at you, shaming you, or insulting you, if you do not like it, tell the people in your life to stop hurting you, and expect that they do it. And this includes your parents, your teachers, your bosses, your friends, your uncles, your spouses and everybody. Always remember, *nobody has the right to violate your boundaries; so, demand and expect that they stop.* If you are serious about awakening and empowerment, there can be no compromise here. Assert your boundaries. Stop the hurt.

That is all I have to say for this chapter. Remember, you need boundaries. To establish them, change your thinking about their importance (i.e. establish right thought in this regard) and begin to assert, expect, and demand boundaries. As a final word, know that you do not have to do this all at once. So, do not feel overwhelmed. If you do feel overwhelmed, take a few deep breathes. You do not have to successfully assert all necessary boundaries all at once in order to get started on a path of authentic spiritual awakening, but you do have to start. It is particularly important not only because if you don't assert boundaries ongoing damage to your physical unit will defeat your ability to awaken, but also because, and this is important, *the more spiritual progress you make, the more aware you become, the more energy flows in your body, the more sensitive and easy to hurt you will be.* If you do not start learning to assert your boundaries now you will eventually find yourself blocked by violence and negativity, and bumped off the path. Either you will give up and go away, you will harden (i.e. desensitize) yourself to prevent feeling hurt all the time (a hardening that, by definition, is the opposite of awakening), or you will collapse into a neurotic (and possibly psychotic) mess.

None of those outcomes is acceptable, so take this advice seriously. Boundaries are important. If you want to make spiritual progress, learn about them, assert them, and defend them.

Visualization Magic

In the past few lessons, we have talked about the importance of boundaries, breathing, will, and intent. These are all important ideas and techniques and if you want to make progress forward, you need to keep them to hand in your spiritual "tool belt." In this week's lesson, I want to continue our discussion of basic technique by looking at the importance of visualization.

As I have noted elsewhere,[91] visualization is critical to spiritual awakening and activation. If the physical body is a vehicle for spirit (which it is), and if your monadic soul gets into the body in order to drive around physical creation (which it does), then *visualization is the wheel that you use to steer the vehicle.*[92] When it comes to driving the physical vehicle, visualization is what gets you where you want to go.

The idea behind the spiritual magic of visualization is very simple, and identical to the idea of prayer (i.e. send a request to the universe) and/or "attraction" (i.e. be a little bit more forceful with the request) that has been "recently" popularized.[93] If you want something, put an image of it in your head, and keep that image there. Doing so will begin to draw the energies necessary to manifest your intent. It is a question of *as above in*

---

[91] Sharp, The Great Awakening: Concepts and Techniques for Successful Spiritual Practice.

[92] Actually, visualization is *much more* than a simple "steering wheel" for your physical body. As we discuss at more advanced levels of study, visualization/vision/intent shapes reality.

[93] I say "recently" in scare quotes here because this notion of attraction has been around for a long time. When you "attract," basically you make a "Disney" wish (e.g. I want more money), visualize an outcome, and then trust (have faith) that the "cosmos" will send it to you. This is exactly the same thing, and about equally as effective, as getting on your knees, praying to God and hoping "he" will grant your wishes, which is to say—mostly ineffective because it fails to appreciate the true nature of Consciousness and the true parameters of its interaction with creation. And for the record, Consciousness is present everywhere; everything is Consciousness. Consciousness acts through others; consciousness acts through you. If you want prayer, attraction, and visualization to work, you have to get behind and own your own intentions. In other words, do not put your power (which is God's power) into the hands of God. If you do that, you are just undermining God's power to change. By default, that does not work. So, do not do it.

consciousness, so below in matter, as I like to say. Energy follows intent, and since visualization is a focused and easy-to-maintain form of intent, visualization is the *magical key* that steers the vehicle. If you want to engage the process of awakening and empowerment, if you want to make the shift, then visualization and intent are key.

We spoke briefly about visualization in LP Workbook One, particularly around the concept of **Boundary Visualizations.**[94] Boundary visualizations are visualizations that help you establish and reinforce personal safe zones; but expansions and refinements of our understanding are still necessary. For example, one question that should emerge at this point is that if visualization is the magical key to awakening and activation, then how do you do it right. Perhaps better questions at this point would be how do you control the direction of manifestation and how do you increase the power of your visualizations. In this regard, *clear images are the key to precise and powerful visualization.* A visualization is a vision, an image. If you want the vision to pan out, you have to have a clear image in mind. This is not as hard as you might think. It is really just a question of practice. The more you practice visualization, the more clear and precise your images will be.

A question that might arise at this point is, how do you practice visualization? That is easy. You practice it by doing it. Close your eyes and visualize a picture, an object, or an outcome in your reality. If you have trouble doing that, start simple. Hold a simple object like a glass or a book in your hand, look at it for a few seconds noticing its shape, color, and texture, and then close your eyes; but, keep the image in your mind. If there is nothing there to begin with, do not worry. Keep practicing. Do this a few times a day for a few weeks and your power to visualize will develop and grow.

---

[94] For a rundown of boundary visualizations, and many other LP visualizations, see http://www.thelightningpath.com/meditations-and-mantras/

Clear, concrete, and precise images in your mind are not the only requirement for successful visualization. Another requirement is *persistence*. If you want your visualizations to work, you have to hold them in your mind for extended periods, especially when the thing you want to manifest is complex, or there is resistance involved. As far as keeping a persistent visualization in mind, that is simply a question of discipline. If you want to be successful, you have to find some way to remind yourself each day what it is you want to manifest, and you have to repeatedly and clearly visualize the outcome. It is not rocket science; it is just a question of clarity and persistence. You can use sticky notes, objects (e.g. pictures, strings), or even apps to remind you to visualize. You can also set aside a certain amount of time each day for the visualizations. Really, you can do whatever you want. There are no hard and fast rules here so explore! Find techniques and strategies that work for you, and use those.

Of course, this all seems sensible and straightforward and in a way it is; but two things can get in your way of clear and persistent vision. **First**, depending on the training you got as a child, you may or may not have developed the ability to visualize. Visualization is a skill, not a talent or a gift, and this skill needs to be developed. Typically, it is developed with *right brain* sorts of activities like music, art, dance, game play, certain types of math, creative writing, and so on. If you have a hard time with visualization, and if you look back on your childhood and see a lack of creative training, know it is never too late to start. If you want to develop your ability to visualize, use the practice suggestions above, but do more as well. Pick up a musical instrument, dance, sing, draw, play games, practice (close your eyes and imagine beaches and warm breezes), color in a book, move (e.g., yoga, judo, tai-chi), and so on.

And please, take this advice seriously. I am not recommending these things to fill up space on this page. I am recommending them because visualization is important and if you want to learn to visualize, heck if you just want to be a whole human being, you need balanced development of your brain. Balanced development of your physical brain is an essential prerequisite of full human expression. It is also an essential requirement for spiritual advancement not only for this beginner level but also for advanced level graduate experiences as well.

Besides lack of creative training as a child, the **second** thing that can get in the way of visualization is simple lack of a good vision. This is particularly true when it comes to the early stages of the awakening, activation, and ascension process. Without direct experience of each of these aspects of spiritual realization, the concepts are all a bit abstract. What is worse, things you read are often not much help. There is a lot of misunderstanding and confusion when it comes to spiritual awakening, activation, and so on. The problem for us here is, if we do not understand what it is we are visualizing, or if we only have abstract ideas, we cannot come up with an effective/accurate visualization. Visualizing forward movement on a spiritual path is not like visualizing clear and concrete things like a new job, a new house, a wedding ring, or whatever. What does "spiritual awakening" look like, after all? It can seem like a real conundrum, especially for those just starting out; but it is not an obstacle. You should already know one very powerful awakening visualization, which is the **Water Glass Metaphor** mentioned in LP Workbook One.[95] To make the metaphor a visualization, simply replace the word "metaphor" with the word "visualization." To do the **Water Glass Visualization**, simply visualize your body as an empty glass of water and visualize consciousness as water pouring into the glass. Visualize the glass (your physical body) filling you up from bottom to top. When it is full, if you want, visualize the water

---

[95] The water glass metaphor is a metaphor used to describe the processes of re-connection (a.k.a. enlightenment/awakening) as viewed from the perspective of the physical unit. The visualization shows water (i.e. Consciousness) filling the glass (i.e. the physical body). See https://www.youtube.com/watch?v=D_5oZV4CuIE and also www.thespiritwiki.com/Water_Glass_Metaphor/.

flowing over the edge of the glass and spilling out into the world around you.[96] Do this visualization as many times a day as you can remember and before you know it, consciousness will be expanding into your body and your whole world will change.

As you can see, the water glass visualization is clear and concise. It is also very powerful. Do not doubt that for a second! The Water Glass Visualization will help you awaken, activate and transform very rapidly. Even better, you can use it right now without knowing all the details of awakening and activation up front. Be careful though, and remember my earlier advice. If things get too hairy, scary, and confusing, *stop intending, stop visualizing,* and take some time off to talk, process, integrate and ground the shifts and transformations. Remember, <u>this is not a race</u> and there is no reward for finishing ahead of others. Slow and steady is the safest way to go.

That is all there is to it. When you are ready to get started on the process of awakening and empowerment, visualize and recite an awakening mantra (e.g. "I wish to move forward) *and* use some variant of the water glass visualization to initiate the process. As a final warning, avoid straying too far from the meditation and visualization guidance provided by the LP teachings, at least at the start. In particular, do not use meditations and mantras you find from other locations unless you fully understand them. Anybody can cobble together a mantra and visualization, but not everybody knows exactly what it is they are doing, and not everybody has good intent. Even slight misconceptions or subtly shifted visuals can lead to unintended and even disastrous consequences. Remember, *you are playing with the fire of Consciousness here.* You are playing with the power of Creation. Be cautious; be careful;

---

[96] You can modify the water glass visualization it different ways. One example is to visualize light and make it more "spiritual" by visualizing *light* streaming <u>into</u> your body through your head (i.e. crown chakra) and dispersing, in scintillating diamond-like patterns, throughout the various "pathways" (i.e. nerve cells, arteries, etc.) of your body. Use with caution.

discern.

Before moving on, I have a few general things to say about this process of visualization and intent. **First of all**, be aware that visualization and intent, as practiced on the LP is different from the venal "attraction" popularized by *The Secret* in a number of key ways. **For one**, visualization as practiced on the LP is not a passive process—it is an active and willful one. When you visualize and intend, you do not sit back and pray for attraction to kick in or something to be given to you, you make a demand of the universe and you work your ass off to get it. When you visualize you say, "I want this and I want this now," but you have to use your hands and legs to help get it as well. It is necessary. If you think the universe is just going to drop prosperity down on your head, you have another thing coming. If you are one of the lucky few to be born into wealth or win a lottery, bully for you; but the rest of the planet needs willful intent and active, engaged creation. Make a demand of the universe and push the issue.

Second, it is important to recognize, visualization and intent are not **profane** processes, they are a deep and essential spiritual process. To *profane* something means, according to Merriam-Webster, to

> 1) treat (something sacred) with abuse, irreverence, or contempt : desecrate; or 2) to debase by a wrong, unworthy, or vulgar use.

To use intent/visualization to attract prosperity is a profane use of the magic of creation. You can do it, and that is fine. There is nothing particularly wrong with that, unless all you do is exploit creations' magic for personal gain without regard for others, and at the expense of collective or planetary wellbeing. If you do that, you are a threat to the survival of humanity and the planet. Visualization and intent are equally about awakening, activation, ascension, happiness, living a calm and happy life, global justice, and so on.[97] You have to remember, it is not just about you. Remember, this is about awakening and empowerment of you, of your community, and of this entire planet. Attract financial prosperity if you like, but be sure to put the spiritual side of this spiritual technique at the demanding forefront of your intent and visualization regime. The goal is not to live a rich and happy life, in a financial sense (although everybody should be able to do that); *the goal is to realize fully your essential divinity.* The goal is to awaken, activate, and ascend. You are wasting your life and blowing any opportunities to help (with awakening, activation, and ascension) if you just focus on money, profit, and all the other goals of our globalized capitalist system.

Third, and most importantly, keep in mind this truth, visualization is a positive process, always. That is, not thinking about something, not visualizing it, pretending something does not exist, ignoring it, sticking your head in the proverbial sand, what we might call, with tongue in cheek, **negative visualization,**[98] does not work! Just because you refuse to think about something does not mean it will not happen. Nobody runs around thinking they are going to get hit and killed by a drunk driver, but some people do get killed. Pretend all you

---

[97] Of course, you can try to realize prosperity through simple attraction, but in most cases that will probably fail, especially right now when the economic system of this planet is so out of balance and skewed (read *Rocket Scientists' Guide to Money and the Economy*). I am not saying this to discourage your attempts to attract prosperity; by all means try! I am just saying, under the current global economic regime, the gap between rich and poor is increasing, with more poor people appearing all the time. Try to attract prosperity all you want, but if you fail, if things do not work out, do not blame yourself, the universe, or visualization. Blame the people responsible for the predatory economic system that disadvantages so many, while privileging so few. If you do not place responsibility at the footstep of those responsible, you will end up depressed, debilitated, and disempowered. Moreover, do not worry if prosperity does not work out. As "the shift" progresses and the planet transforms, global prosperity for all will come, so hang in there. In the meantime, keep the idea of prosperity in the back of your mind, but remember why you are here.

[98] Negative visualization is the blocking out of ideas or images in the mind, as if pretending something does not exist necessary means it does not. For more on negative visualization, see http://www.thespiritwiki.com/Negative_Visualization/.

want, but pretending a thing does not exist, or avoiding thinking about it, does not mean it does not, or will not exist. Creation is *always* an active process. Creation *always* requires an image and intent. I cannot, could not, and would not, in a million years, underestimate the importance of this key creative principle. Creation is active and if you want to create you have to actively engage. If you erase the image, you erase your influence on reality.

Here is an example that should be increasingly close to heart. Just because you refuse to think about war in the Middle East, or war in America, does not mean war will not happen in those places. In fact, not thinking about the Middle East, or America... specifically, not throwing your intent firmly down on the side of peace, can facilitate war. If you do not actively dispel images of war and violence, if you do not consciously dismiss the fighting (and the fighters), if you do not consciously intend for global peace to occur, if you just stick your head in the stand and pretend there is no danger, then there are no countervailing intents! You have to remember, there are many people painting on the canvas of this Earth, and you are just one. If all the hawks in the US are busy visualizing and intending war in the Middle East, and you engage in wishful non-thinking, pretending that out of sight means out of manifestation, then all the hawks will get their way because nobody is intending an opposite reality. Pay attention to this next statement. Make sure you understand it, and keep it always in mind: *If you are not drawing energy toward a reality that you want, the intent of those who are will "trump" your blissful non-attention.* The universe works this way. Creation is an active process, always. *If you do not apply the force of intention, those who do will always get their way.*

Also, keep in mind the fact that that visualization is not just about attraction. Attraction works hand in hand with repulsion. Put another way, visualization and intent work any way you like. If you do not like something, if you do not like somebody, you have the power and ability to draw a boundary and exclude.

This is true at a collective level (i.e. if billions put aside notions of good fighting evil and all other justifications for war and conflict, conflict would end pretty quickly) and an individual level. If you do not want war in the Middle East, think about the soldiers going away. If you do not want some violent and abusive bully in your circle of friends, draw a visual circle (i.e. a boundary) around yourself and push the bully out, gently and with compassion if you like. If you do not like violence, put a big X in your mind along with the words "NO MORE VIOLENCE." You will be surprised at just how good this **Law of Repulsion**[99] works for you, especially as more and more people put aside their ideologically programmed aversion to it[100] and get on with the end times program.

The process is simple. There is no excuse not to do it. Use will and intent to attract what you want (for example, utopia) but also use will and intent to repulse what you do not (like war, famine, and greed). It is not about morality; it is about keeping yourself and your family protected, and saving the planet.

That is all I have on visualization, for now. As a final summary, I assume that at this point you have read *The Great Awakening: Concepts and Techniques for Successful Spiritual Practice*, have gone over the basic spiritual concept and techniques in that book, and now have a strong and solid grasp of the basics. I also hope that you have been making intent statements (i.e. "I wish to move forward") since the start. In order to add fuel to the process, add constant visualization to your awakening

---

[99] The *Law of Repulsion* is a law of intent/visualization that states removal of unpleasant realities requires active and engaged repulsion. For more, see http://www.thespiritwiki.com/Law_of_Repulsion.

[100] By this I mean, you are taught not to repulse. From a very early age the priests and the pundits and the spiritual "teachers" discourage you from pushing things away. You are taught to accept whatever life sends your way because it is part of your "lesson plan," part of the "checkboard," or part of God's plan. There is a "light side" and a "dark side" and that is just the way God wants it to be. You have to accept the bad with the good. Shit happens. Just put up, toughen up, shut up, and accept. It is all horseshit though. You do not have to accept anything "life" sends your way and in fact, you should not. You should realize, this is just a euphemism for being boundary-less and open to exploitation. Stop accepting the bullshit. Reject it, revile it, and push it away with all your visualization might.

process, now. Start with the water glass visualization and use more advanced archetypes and visualizations provided for you as you progress along the path. Finally, always remember this: the best progress is made if you are persistent and consistent. Recite your awakening mantra and do the water glass visualization for a few seconds several times a day and it will not take too long before noticeable shifts begin to occur.

Additional Obstacles

In the last section, we explored visualization. There we learned that visualization is a key aspect of the spiritual process. If you do not visualize and intend, nothing is going to happen. In fact, and very important for you to understand, if you do not visualize and intend, you will easily become the victim of those who do.

Prior to our discussion of visualization, we also discussed alignment, intent, the importance of boundaries, staying the course, and so on. Each of these discussions has been important not only because they illustrate key ideas and concepts, but also because these discussions have highlighted the fact that on any authentic path of awakening and activation there are obstacles and challenges that must be overcome if you want to move forward. There is no way around them. You clear the obstacles and challenges or you stay stuck in the mud of "normal" consciousness.

Unfortunately, the obstacles and challenges outlined so far in this workbook, and in the previous ones, are just a short itemization of a longer list of challenges and obstacles we all face. We will be spending a lot of time examining obstacles and helping you clear them as we progress through these materials. In this chapter, I want to continue the process by identifying and talking about some psychological and emotional obstacles that you might face, and that you need to recognize and clear if you are going to move forward.

One of first psychological obstacles you might face is what we might want to call a **cognitive wall**. *A cognitive wall is an intellectual wall between you and an idea that prevents you from connecting with/understanding the idea.* You will know you have a cognitive wall if you pick up a normal book[101] and

---

[101] And by normal I mean not a specialist textbook or an advanced reading in an area you know nothing about. If you pick up a specialist book with a lot of jargon and technical details you aren't familiar with, it is not a cognitive

simply cannot access the meaning of the words on the page. You will see the words, you will read them, but you will not be able to understand them, even when they are simple and straightforward. Cognitively, you will withdraw to another space. As you drift away, the words will lose all meaning.[102] If this happens to you, do not feel bad. We all have cognitive walls and we all use them from time to time to avoid things we do not want to think about, talk about, or deal with. It is the nature of the beast, so to speak. It is no big deal so long as you learn to recognize the ones you have and tear them down so they do not block your progress. If you recognize that you have them, and you recognize when they come up, you can take steps to bring them down. Tearing them down is not altogether difficult. If there is a cognitive wall preventing you from connecting with some ideas, recognize it is there and power through it. It might take a bit of practice, and you may have to read the same passages over a few times before you have cleared the way, but you can do it. It is simply a matter of identifying the wall and clawing your way through. Be persistent and patient and you will make it through.

A cognitive wall is often, though not always, the result of an unconscious desire to avoid. Sometimes you can experience problems connecting to information sources for other reasons, like for example low blood sugar or lack of sleep. If your brain does not have the energy/nutrition it needs to function, or if you are exhausted from lack of sleep, you will have trouble

---

block, it is a lack of training.

[102] Of course, you may not like to admit to yourself that your mind is closed and you are glossing over the words. So, you may choose to delude yourself into thinking you have heard, understood, and grounded the message even when you have not. Do not kid yourself. We all have cognitive walls. We develop them on our own as a practiced method of avoidance *and* they are put there, sometimes consciously, usually unconsciously, by parents, teachers, the media, the churches of this world, and so on. They are put there to prevent us from connecting and seeing the truth and they are powerful in the resistance they provide. They are also relatively easy to dispel *if* you are aware they are there. If you know they are there, it is a simple process of powering your way through. Just focus on the idea, study, and reread until you understand. Do not kid yourself and you will have no problem clearing your way through the blockage.

connecting with, grounding, and process information. Therefore, make sure you eat well and get lots of sleep.

Cognitive walls arise especially when materials are challenging to you personally. You may cognitively withdraw from materials when you are asked to think about things you do not want to think about, like for example how you may be abusing others in your life, or do things you do not want to do, like stop exploiting Asian children for shareholder profit. Cognitive walls may also exist because of ideology and indoctrination, i.e., when your consciousness has been deliberately turned away from consideration of certain things. The latter happens a lot with spiritual discourse, especially with those who have scientific training. Mention the word "God" or "angels" to a trained materialist, for example, and their mind may wander, their eyes might gloss over, and they may react with intellectual or emotional violence as they try and put the idea down. Of course, materialists are not the only ones with cognitive walls that prevent them from having an open mind about certain things. Some Christians, for example, shut down if they see the word "tarot." I could rehearse the various ideas that invoke cognitive walls here, but the point is not to draw out a long list of our cognitive biases, the point is to highlight the existence of these walls so that you can be aware they exist and on guard when they come up. If they do come up, put effort into working through them. If there is one thing you have to have when moving forward, it is an open mind. Consciousness is nothing but ideas. *If you close your mind off to ideas, you close your mind to Consciousness.* Of course, having an open mind does not mean being an airhead. Having an open mind does not mean you have to agree with all the ideas that you see on a page or that float through your head, but you do have to be open to consideration, at least while you are a student. If your mind is closed, you will never learn the things you need to learn, put aside the biases you need to put aside, or develop the abilities you need to develop, to make a strong connection. By all means have an open mind, but don't put aside your critical sensibility.

Besides putting up a cognitive wall, another way of avoiding challenging ideas and expectations is by dodging them through dissembling and distraction. Transpersonal psychologists call this **spiritual bypassing**.[103] Spiritual bypassing occurs, for example, when we tell ourselves that we are OK yet distract ourselves from ideas and realizations that might suggest otherwise. We distract ourselves by using *things* (like "spiritual" crystals), *ideas* (like peace and love), *actions* (working, exercising, volunteering), and even *places* (Facebook, the local bar) to avoid having to deal with the issues, blockages, sins, and wounds.[104] We do so both as a form of presentation and avoidance. We present to the world an image of ourselves as we would like to think we are (and as we would like others to think we are) and we involve ourselves with things, ideas, actions, and places that distract us from the hard truths of our realities. We rub Tibetan singing bowls, wear crystals, attend spiritual shows, go to church, read books from the latest guru, and do whatever we can to avoid dealing with the issues. By putting on a show, we convince others and ourselves that we are doing, or have done, the work. We use the "right" symbols, right words, and right products as a form of escapism, and we do it to avoid the more serious job of healing, alignment, awakening, activation, and so on.

Individuals who are practiced at spiritual bypassing will have a hard time with LP materials because these materials provide no opportunity for spiritual bypassing. LP materials are clear, grounded, connected, and to the point. Truths are stated precisely and if you are paying attention, there is no opportunity

---

[103] http://www.thespiritwiki.com/Spiritual_Bypassing/.

[104] Mentor note: You can easily spot a spiritual bypasser by their ostentatious display of "spiritual" symbol and product. One woman we (my wife and I) knew had angels buzzing around at her front door, i.e. she had signs and statues of angels on display in her entranceway. As we quickly learned, this woman was bypassing to avoid considering her own toxicity, vis a vis her oldest male child.

to ignore what is being said. Unlike so many "self-help" style spiritual books, there is no sugar coating. Either you face the truth, or you do not. This will be a challenge for some. Those who are used to spiritual bypassing, or who have established cognitive walls, will look to find the same fluffy, bypass friendly, emptiness here as they find elsewhere. When they do not find it, they will either tune out and go glassy eyed (cognitive wall) or they will violently, and often fearfully, reject the materials. They may issue the rejection physically by actually throwing the book down, or they may engage in a violent emotional/psychological rejection. They will come up with all sorts of arguments to diminish/discredit the work so they do not have to listen to and/or ground the ideas; and, it is not that hard to do. Human beings have a highly evolved capacity for self-delusion, and they can delude themselves about anything. If a human decides they do not want to know something, there are a hundred things they can do to bypass that knowing.

Unlike a cognitive wall which is relatively easy to get through once you recognize it is there, spiritual bypassing can be more difficult. The primary problem for most people is recognizing that they are doing it. It is a negative process (i.e. avoidance) hidden within a positive activity of some sort. The challenges arise because the bypassing is something we do to protect ourselves. Spiritual bypassing is an **Awareness Reduction Mechanism**[105] that we invoke as a way to defend ourselves from anxiety, negative emotions (guilt/shame), fear, and/or threat. Spiritual bypassing is an active process that allows us to direct attention (our own, and the attention of others) away from difficult issues which cause us painful disjuncture and stress. As we redirect attention, our awareness of difficult and challenging issues is reduced. This reduction of awareness works to reduce anxiety/fear/distress in the short term. However, in the long

---

[105] Awareness Reduction Mechanisms (ARMs), what psychologists typically call defense mechanisms, are strategies that the bodily ego can use to reduce awareness of itself, its physical and mental condition, the "room" that it's in, and the condition of its life. See http://www.thespiritwiki.com/Awareness_Rediction_Mechanisms/

term, it may lead to recalcitrant blockage, illness, and even death as the body fails under the strain and toxic burden of pathological avoidance.

The easiest way to overcome spiritual bypassing is to figure out what you are afraid of, and what causes you pain. It could be many things from guilt and shame to actual, Catholic instilled fear of punishment/damnation. Once you have identified whatever fear/anxiety is causing you to avoid/bypass, face it. Look at it, examine it, roll it around in your head, look for its source, etc. As you do this, it is worthwhile reminding yourself of the basic messages of the LP, which are love everyone, accept everyone, heal everyone, provide for everyone, align everyone, and clean up this horrible mess of a planet, for the benefit of everyone. There is absolutely nothing in the messages of the LP to warrant any kind of fearful, anxious, rejection. There are no threats of damnation, there are no subtle exclusionary dogmas, we do not put anybody down (though we do have high standards for Truth), and we put into practice everything we say. You may decide you do not like this message, but that should not stop you from keeping an open mind and taking a closer look. In any case, whether you stay focused here or move on to something else, it is important to overcome cognitive blockages and put aside spiritual bypassing. Progress forward is impossible if you do not.

So far we have discussed cognitive walls and spiritual bypassing. A third area of possible challenge, **active resistance**, is a bit more difficult than even spiritual bypassing. Active resistance involves actively and consciously working to reject whatever it is you do not want to see. As an example, active resistance may occur as you begin to get into the intermediate LP materials, and in particular the cosmology and theology of the Lightning Path, as introduced in The Book of Light Volume One. There is no other way to say it here, but in the context of some of the beliefs we are taught as part of what I would call **Old World**

Spirituality,[106] LP teachings are blasphemous, and the blasphemy can be a challenge. If you have been trained in old world spiritualties, or even new world science, you may have strong visceral, emotional, fearful, or even angry reactions to some of the things you hear me say. If you have these reactions, you may actively reject, dismiss, and even go out of your way to disprove.

The reasons for these reactions and resistance are not that hard to uncover. Either you have an emotional attachment to the concepts you are protecting, or you are filled with fear, anxiety, and worry that if you think or do the wrong things, you will be punished, ostracized, and excluded. As for an emotional attachment to ideas, these happen all the time. Consider the **Father God**[107] that the Christian Church pimps. Some (exactly how many is a research question) people attach to this God as a surrogate for earthly fathers who were absent, unavailable, and unattached. That is, children attach to Father God in an often desperate and ultimately futile[108] attempt to meet needs unmet by their absent physical father. When individuals have such an emotional attachment to the concept of Father God, challenges to the concept may be experienced as threats to their emotional and psychological wellbeing. As a result of the threat, they may resist, often quite aggressively.[109]

Of course, deep psychological attachments to old world ideas

---

[106] http://www.thespiritwiki.com/Old_World_Spirituality/.

[107] Father God refers to the paternal personification of God offered to the masses by priests of Western ecclesiastical institutions. Father God is offered as a surrogate/opportunistic replacement for real fathers who are emotionally unavailable, unattached, or absent from an offspring's childhood as the result of war, work, abandonment, etc. For more see http://www.thespiritwiki.com/Father_God/.

[108] Despite what foolish priests might want you to believe, a celestial patriarch can never replace a real, live, embodied, attached, loving, attentive, and protective human father.

[109] From a therapeutic/mentor perspective, when an individual has an emotional attachment to a concept like Father God, it best not to poke too hard. Doing so only activates their defenses and exposes you to forms of violence and assault. Better to deal with the underlying emotional dynamic first.

are not the only reason we actively resist. It often comes down to simple fear arising from abuse in childhood.

As children, we may have been beaten and abused simply for making a mistake, failing to follow a rule, or even saying what we really think/feel.

The abuse can be physical, or more likely, it can be psychological and emotional. If we associate being wrong with punishment, we may come to harbor deep, unconscious anxiety and fear about doing or thinking the wrong thing. If we do harbor deep fears and anxieties about being wrong, then we may forcefully resist new ideas simply because to accept the ideas implies that we are wrong in our current thinking and action, and the idea of being wrong invokes deep fear and anxiety. We react to this fear and anxiety by actively resisting new ideas.

If this is you, if you find yourself forcefully resisting new ideas because of emotional attachment to old ones or anxiety about shifting into new ways of being, then the best advice I have for you is this: chill out. Relax. Calm down. It is no big deal to be wrong and I am not forcing you to believe or think anything you do not want to believe, or think. Be cool about it. While I certainly believe everything that I say, you do not have to believe anything if you do not want to. Nobody is forcing you to do anything and nobody is going to condemn you for being wrong, or making a mistake. You can stay exactly where you are for as long as you like, and that is fine. Nobody, except maybe your own higher Self,[110] is forcing you to move forward, so take a deep breath, relax, and think about things. That is all. Regardless of whether you choose to remain on this path or not, *it never hurts to expand your mind by considering new*

---

[110] Saying "higher Self" is a bit redundant since capitalizing the "S" of self indicates I am speaking about the higher consciousness (i.e. Consciousness with a capital "C") that animates your physical unit. Self, but not self, is higher consciousness. Until I feel there is general understanding of the difference between self and Self, I may or may not choose to say just Self, or higher Self.

concepts and ideas. A little extra knowledge and self-awareness is always a good thing! If you decide it is not for you, then it is not for you. That is all there is to it.

At this point, we have talked about cognitive walls, spiritual bypassing, and emotionally charged resistance to new ideas as possible blockages to moving forward on the Path. **A fourth thing** that might cause issues is **overly inflated expectations** and the belief in **spiritual fixes**.[111] Depending on what you have read in the past about spirituality and enlightenment, you may be expecting too much. Many people have unreasonable expectations about what happens on a spiritual path, and when you listen to them, they pass these expectations on to you to the point where you may think that a little deep breathing, a little transcendental meditation, a little "magic dust," and a little intent is all you need for total enlightenment. While this is true to an extent (persistent intent to move forward is the key to spiritual success, breathing is critical, and a little "magic dust" never really hurt anybody), it may take more time than you think because there may be a lot for you to do. You may have past life fear and trauma to deal with. You may have "this life" fear and trauma to heal. You may be filled with wrong thinking and spiritual misconceptions that prevent you from awakening and activating. You may have emotional blockages that prevent you from engaging ideas. You may have psychological damage from trauma and abuse in your life. In other words, you may have learning, healing, and clearing to do as you move yourself forward. Unfortunately, all these things (and more) can take time. Therefore, be reasonable with your expectations. Unreasonable expectations about what to expect and how fast you can move can interfere with ongoing progress. If you expect fireworks, and if things do not shake out for you fast enough, you may simply give up and start looking for your next instant spiritual fix.

---

[111] http://www.thespiritwiki.com/Spiritual_Fix

And, that's not good. If you run around looking for instant spiritual fixes, you are going to be running in circles your whole life. There are no instant fixes. Of course, this is not to say that rapid, even instantaneous, spiritual transformation cannot occur. It can. Total visions of reality, total realizations of identity, and total enlightenments are possible, particularly in moments of strong connection; but even if you suddenly realize the full and awesome truth that you are, in fact, God, you still have to take that in, process it, and ground it. The realizations and enlightenments that come along this path are big, and there are lots of them. This is because the *Consciousness that you connect to is vast, much bigger than the tiny little brain in your head can handle all at once.* Not only that, your brain, your bodily ego, and all the structures of your bodily consciousness can be damaged by assault and abuse throughout your life. This damage, which can make it hard to contain higher Consciousness, takes time and effort to heal. You cannot just rub a crystal singing bowl and heal childhood sexual abuse. You cannot clear away the limiting ideology of old energy archetypes and replace them with shiny new ones in an instant. There is real spiritual work involved. How much is hard to say because it depends.[112] The point is, manage your expectations so you can avoid disappointment and distraction. Do not expect instant shifts into glorious ascended existence. Embrace the shifts joyfully when they do occur, but be prepared to buckle down and work because there are challenges and struggles ahead, and these are going to take time to resolve.

---

[112] It depends on how open you are. It depends on how much time you put into it. It depends on how damaged you have become. It depends upon what resistances you face. It depends upon the *real* support that you are able to muster. Heck, it can even depend on the amount of sleep that you get and the type of food that you eat. Getting better sleep and eating better food will help speed you on your way. The truth is, there are many factors that can influence how efficiently you move down the path, so it is hard to predict; however, predicting is not the point here.

Conclusion

Thus, we come to an end of LP Workbook Three. In this book, we have discussed intent, breathing, boundaries, visualization, alignment, obstacles, and a host of other important concepts. The concepts we have discussed here are important building blocks for awakening and activation. Keep in mind, what you got here was just the basics. The information provided here and ongoing provides an intellectual and emotional precursor to the real work of connection. Beyond this, *you need the meditations, visualizations, and real connection experiences of intermediate and advanced study to move yourself forward.* Do not worry; we will get to that. In the meantime, don't forget your awakening mantras and visualizations. These are what will move you forward towards awakening, connection, and activation experiences, so recite/visualize them whenever you can.

Speaking of intermediate and advanced levels of study, at the next level of study we take a much closer look at what it means to be a spiritual person, and we do that by placing emphasis <u>not</u> on your soul but on your body. As you will learn throughout your study, your soul, your higher consciousness, is already super bright and super powerful. Your soul, your monadic self, is never going to be any less bright, powerful, blissful, or aware than it already is. There is, in other words, nothing wrong with your soul. The same cannot be said for your physical body/mind. *Despite what anybody else has told you, your physical body/mind is incredibly fragile and easy to damage.* The truth is, even a single mean word can destroy self-esteem and damage the ego to the point of requiring difficult and challenging repair. This is no laughing matter. Every day people die long and horrible deaths because of the toxicity and abuse they have experienced as children and young adults. More to the point, you cannot make spiritual progress if you do not attend to the health and wellbeing of your body and mind.

This is important, so pay attention. As we will see in the next workbook, the problem of spirituality is not a problem of morality, philosophy, karma, or whatever. In the context of LP teachings, *the problem of spirituality is a problem of the body.* The problem of spirituality is a problem of getting the body into a state where it can properly handle and express the bliss, power and awareness of Consciousness. Unfortunately, getting the body into a state where it can handle higher consciousness can be a problem. For reasons outlined throughout the LP corpus, this world is not particularity open to the true expression of Consciousness in the body. In fact, quite the opposite is true. Across the board, this planet is hostile to Consciousness. From the ideas in our head, through the actions that we take, the environments that we create, and the damage that has been done, we do not live in a world that honors and accepts Consciousness. We live in a world that diminishes and rejects Consciousness. It is time to change that. On the LP we take a serious look at what it takes (i.e. things you need to do, and the changes you need to make) to make the physical body a proper and accommodating vessel for higher consciousness. As you will see, it is not rocket science; similarly, it is definitely not business as usual. Consciousness is Consciousness and, as explained in *The Book of Light*, Consciousness is the primary reality of this universe. As such Consciousness is powerful, bright, forceful, aware, super-intelligent, perfectly aligned, and non-compromising, to name a few characteristics. As we will see, it is not a question of soul lessons or life paths. It is a question of spiritual health, spiritual fitness, and bodily repair. If you want to expand Consciousness into the body, you need to prepare the vessel. It is to a deeper consideration of this that we turn to in LP Workbook Four.

Michael Sharp

March 7, 2017

Organizing Your Workgroup

As mentioned in the introduction to this book, this workbook is designed to facilitate individual study *and* classroom based exploration. If you are interested in doing spiritual workgroups, you can easily manage the group using the tools and techniques provided here. My suggestion is that you get members to read a single chapter before the group meets. When the group meets the class can discuss the individual questions and key concepts.

If your workgroup or classroom is small, say less than eight people, you can discuss the questions and concepts as a whole. However, if your group is larger than eight, consider breaking up the larger group into smaller groups of no more than six people. Do not expect each group to deal with all the questions. Break the question and concepts up and assign one or more (as necessary) to each individual or group.

If this is a formal classroom situation, the individual groups should pick a transcriber, someone who will write the group's thoughts down. The transcriber is responsible for accurately representing what the group is thinking. The group also needs to pick a representative, i.e. one who will stand in front of the larger group or class and share the group's discussion. The representative can use the notes of the transcriber, or they can use their own notes so long as they are complete.

As a workgroup facilitator, your job is to walk amongst the groups, listen to what they are saying, and help move their discussion along. Contribute ideas and corrections as necessary. Pay attention to group dynamics. Are some monopolizing the conversation? Do some seem too shy to contribute? Address these issues with compassion and concern. The goal is to create workgroups where everybody is comfortable to speak. To do that you may have to be supportive and encouraging, and you may have to engage in a little psychotherapy.

When it comes to selecting a representative, encourage the

group members to be thoughtful. First, individuals should volunteer. If more than one person expresses an interest in representing the group, *rotate* them. Encourage the group to discuss with the representatives what makes a good representative. For myself, I believe a good representative should be calm, fair (so that all viewpoints are represented), a good speaker, and capable of accepting criticism. Encourage the group to give the representatives *positive* feedback after each presentation. Criticism is acceptable if given with the intent to strengthen and uplift. Criticism intended to undermine and destroy has no place in a functioning spiritual workgroup (or any workgroup for that matter).

Teaching Supports

This workbook comes with various teaching supports, like a twitter feed of ideas and quotes from the book, and quizlets that allow you to study vocabulary and other LP concepts efficiently. For a complete list of available supports, and an overview of LP curriculum, see http://www.thelightningpath.com/fast-path/.

Study Questions[113]

Use these study questions to support your individual study and your workgroup. If you are seeking LP certification, answer these questions in short essays and submit on the LP website.

Alignment

1. According to the text, *alignment* is the most important concept in the LP corpus. In your own words, describe why this concept is so important. Do you feel that you are aligned? If not, identify misalignments.

2. What are some of the reasons the bodily ego might *push* Consciousness away? Examine your own life. Can you find examples where you yourself have pushed awareness away? What were your reasons for doing that?

3. What are the four reasons listed in the text why Consciousness might *pull* away from the physical unit. Once again, examine your life. Do you feel that there are areas in your life where Consciousness may have pulled away?

Two Steps Towards Spiritual Awakening

1. According to the text, there are *two* steps towards spiritual awakening you must take. Name them and discuss their importance.

2. What is the significance of "intent/will" for spiritual awakening? How does the physical unit respond to intent? What have been your personal experiences with will and intent in relation to spiritual awakening and

---

[113] Concepts are worth five points each. Make sure you make at least five relevant and insightful points when you answer the questions.

empowerment?

3. What are some of the challenges involved with maintaining consistent will and intent? What are a couple of strategies/tools listed in the book that you can use to ensure consistent and persistent intent? Can you think of other strategies that might work as well?

4. Intent can be used to initiate awakening and activation, but it can also be used to slow down and stop the process. What sorts of life events or situations can you think of that might require an individual to slow down or even stop the process of awakening and activation for a period of time?

5. What does it mean to say that "you are not the only sparkle of Consciousness that exists on this planet"? What does this have to do with your awakening process and the impact this has on others? What can you do to mitigate the impact and ensure smooth forward movement?

Three Steps on the Ladder

1. Using the metaphor of the room, describe the process of awakening. What determines whether the experience of "turning on the light" is experienced in a positive or negative fashion? Examine your own life. What is the condition of the room? What is your current state of health? Are you willing to face the truth, or do you resist?

2. As noted, activation involves taking action in the world to change the things that need to be changed. Consider your response to the previous question. What sort of actions do you think you need to take to make things right in your world? What are some of the challenges you see that might block you from taking action and making changes?

3. What are six things that you should keep in mind as you struggle to make consistent and persistent forward progress? Do any of these items resonate with you in particular? Can you see others around you (i.e. family, clients) who could benefit from these ideas? Share.

The Importance of Breathing

1. Why is breathing important? From a spiritual perspective, what is deep breathing designed to alleviate? What sorts of conditions trigger the need for breathing?

2. What is the difference between a zenith experience and a nadir experience? Have you had either of these? How did you handle it "in the moment," and subsequently? Share your experiences.

3. Describe the proper technique of breathing. Are there any visualizations you can think of, besides the one provided in the text, that can facilitate the relaxation process? Share.

4. Do some online research and determine some of the physical, psychological, and emotional benefits of deep breathing. Summarize what you find in about 400 – 600 words. Provide links and citations. If you have access, focus on scholarly research.

Staying the Course

1. If the Lightning Path is not about attraction, individual prosperity, reward in the after-life, and acceptance of what is, what is it about? What has been your experience so far? What words would you use to introduce the LP to a potential student or client?

2. What is meant by the phrase, "This is not a one–size-fits-all solution?" What are some issues, challenges, and responsibilities in your own life that might slow you

down or halt your progress forward? What do you do if you are feeling anxious, challenged, frightened, or confused?

3. In addition to taking a break from spiritual study, there is always a danger of being <u>bumped</u> off the path. What are the three things listed that can get you bumped of the path? What are the things listed that you can do to prevent being bumped off the path? Can you think of anything else? Discuss.

Boundaries Redux

1. What are boundaries and why are they important? What are two reasons why, as adults, we do not install and/or maintain boundaries.

2. Examine your own life, and in particular your childhood. How were your boundaries violated in childhood, and by whom? Do you think these boundary violations had an emotional and psychological impact? If so, explain.

3. Keep in mind the body can be hurt by sticks and stones, name calling, screaming, emotional abuse, and so on. Do you believe your current boundaries are sufficient to keep you from being hurt?

4. Consider the importance of boundaries. Do you violate the boundaries of others? If so, in what way? You cannot move forward until you stop those boundary violations, so what are you going to do to stop those boundary violations?

Visualization

1. Assess your ability to visualize. Can you see pictures in your mind's eye when you close your eyes? If not, what are some things you need to do right now to increase your ability to visualize?

2. Visualization is important. In fact, it is a key to the process. However, in order to visualize you need a good vision. What basic awakening visualization and mantra combinations might you recommend to newbies on the spiritual path and why? Is it safe to recommend just any old visualization/mantra? Why?

3. How is LP intent/visualization different from other intent/visualization found in other schools of thought, like *The Secret?* (e.g. not passive, not venal). Explore your own spiritual training. Do you find passive and venal prayer/intent in your traditions? What other differences do you notice? Share.

Potential Obstacles

1. What is a cognitive wall? What are some ways to identify cognitive walls? Why do people build them? How do you overcome them? Do you notice any cognitive walls in your headspace? Share.

2. What is spiritual bypassing? Why do people bypass? Can you think of examples from your own life where you and those you are close to use spiritual bypassing to avoid? Share.

3. How does abuse in childhood lead to resistance to new ideas in adulthood? Explore your own childhood. Has a fear of being wrong and making mistakes been instilled into you?

4. How can overly inflated expectations slow down your spiritual progress? Explore your own biography. Do you have over inflated expectations? If so, where do they come from? Consider parents, teachers, books you have read, television you have watched, etc.

About the Author

Michael Sharp is a Sociologist with a specialization in psychology, religion, occult studies, social inequality, scholarly communication, and critical theory. After a dramatic crown chakra opening caused him to question the materialist foundation of modern science, he began exploring the spiritual and mystical side of life. Recognizing early the presence of elitism and patriarchy in the world's religious and "secret" traditions, he began creating a new, open system of mysticism free of the opportunistic bias in "old energy" systems. The Lightning Path™ is the culmination of his research and work. Visit Michael at http://www.michaelsharp.org.

About the Lightning Path

The Lightning Path (or simply LP for short) is an intellectual, emotional, psychological, and spiritual system of awakening and empowerment (a "mystery school" if you like, but without all the useless mystery) designed to help you get off the sinking ship of the old world and make "the shift" into an awakened, activated, and ascended state of existence. It is sophisticated, powerful, logical, grounded, rational, intellectually and metaphorically rigorous, politically sophisticated, empirically verifiable, authentic, effective, and accessible to everyone regardless of race, class, or gender. No requirements are set for entry and no judgments are made in passage. For more information visit http://www.thelightningpath.com/.

Index

References

Anonymous. "Understanding the Stress Response." *Harvard Health Publications* 2016.

Chu, Sanna. "Is Your Smartphone Created by Slave Labor?" *iDigital Times* 2014.

Sharp, Michael. *The Book of Life: Ascension and the Divine World Order.* St. Albert, AB: Lightning Path Press/Avatar Publications, 2003.

---. *The Book of Light: The Nature of God, the Structure of Consciousness, and the Universe within You.* Vol. one -air. 4 vols. St. Albert, Alberta: Lightning Path Press, 2006.

---. *The Book of Light: The Nature of God, the Structure of Consciousness, and the Universe within You.* Vol. two - water. 4 vols. St. Albert, Alberta: Lightning Path Press, Unpublished.

---. *Dossier of the Ascension: A Practical Guide to Chakra Activation and Kundalini Awakening.* Lightning Path Press, 2003.

---. "Ego Explosion". Sturgeon County, 2014. *The Blog of Michael Sharp.* The Blog of Michael Sharp. <http://www.michaelsharp.org/ego-explosion/>.

---. *The Great Awakening: Concepts and Techniques for Successful Spiritual Practice.* St. Albert, Alberta, Canada: Lightning Path Press, 2007.

---. *Lightning Path Workbook Four - Foundations.* Lightning Path Workbook Series. Ed. Sharp, Michael. Vol. 4. St. Albert, Alberta: Lightning Path Press, Unpublished.

---. *Lightning Path Workbook One - Introduction to Authentic Spirituality.* Lightning Path Workbook Series. Vol. 1. St. Albert, Alberta: Lightning Path Press, 2016.

---. *Lightning Path Workbook Two - Introduction to the Lightning Path.* Lightning Path Workbook Series, St. Albert, Alberta.

---. *The Rocket Scientists' Guide to Authentic Spirituality.* St. Albert, Alberta: Lightning Path Press, 2010.

---. *The Rocket Scientists' Guide to Money and the Economy: Accumulation and Debt.* St Albert, Alberta: Lightning Path Press., 2016.

---. *The Rocket Scientists' Guide to Spiritual Discernment.* St. Albert, Alberta: Lightning Path Press, 2011.

Sosteric, Mike. "Mysticism, Consciousness, Death." *Journal of Consciousness Exploration and Research* 7 11 (2016): 1099-118.

---. "The Science of Ascension: Bodily Ego, Consciousness, Connection". 2016. <https://athabascau.academia.edu/DrS>.

---. "Toxic Socialization." *Socjourn* (2016).